McCaulay's CFA Level I Mock Exam

Philip Martin McCaulay

McCaulay's CFA Level I Mock Exam
ISBN 978-0-557-09945-0
Published in Raleigh, North Carolina, United States of America

© Copyright 2009. All rights reserved. No part of this publication may be reproduced or transmitted in any form or by any means, electronic or mechanical, including photocopy, recording, or any information storage or retrieval system, without permission in written form from the publisher.

CFA®, Chartered Financial Analyst™, CFA Program™, and CFA Institute are trademarks owned by the CFA Institute. CFA Institute does not endorse, promote, review, or warrant the accuracy of the products or services offered by Philip Martin McCaulay. Philip Martin McCaulay is not affiliated with CFA Institute.

McCaulay's CFA Level I Mock Exam
Table of Contents

Morning Exam	Page 1
Morning Exam Answer Key	Page 22
Morning Exam with Answers and Formulas	Page 23
Afternoon Exam	Page 45
Afternoon Exam Answer Key	Page 66
Afternoon Exam with Answers and Formulas	Page 67

About the Book

McCaulay's CFA Level I Sample Mock Exam consists of two 120-question exams, with each exam followed by an answer key and the exam with the answers shown, including the formulas used to derive the numeric answers. The question formats and topic weights are similar to the actual CFA Level I exam. The questions were transformed from the study material in the CFA Institute Program Curriculum available from the CFA Institute. The sample exam is designed to complement the CFA Program curriculum and to facilitate the learning process, not to be used as a substitute for study of the prescribed curriculum. The morning exam is Exam 11 from McCaulay's CFA Level I Practice Exams Volume II of V and the afternoon exam is Exam 21 from McCaulay's CFA Level I Practice Exams Volume III of V.

About the Author

Philip Martin McCaulay has sold thousands of practice exam books and study guides for licensing and credentialing examinations in the fields of pensions, investments, finance, real estate, and massage therapy. He is an actuary with experience on the Society of Actuaries' Education & Examination Committee.

McCaulay's CFA Level I Mock Exam Topic Weights

CFA Level I Topic Area	Percent	Number of Questions	Question Numbers
Ethical and Professional Standards	**15%**	**18**	**1-18**
Quantitative Methods	12%	14	19-32
Economics	10%	12	33-44
Financial Reporting and Analysis	20%	24	45-68
Corporate Finance	8%	10	69-78
Investment Tools (total)	**50%**	**60**	**19-78**
Equity Investments	10%	12	79-90
Derivatives	5%	6	91-96
Fixed Income	12%	14	97-110
Alternative Investments	3%	4	111-114
Asset Classes (total)	**30%**	**36**	**79-114**
Portfolio Management and Wealth Planning	**5%**	**60**	**115-120**
Total	100%	120	1-120

Morning Exam

1. If a member resides in a country with no securities laws or regulations and does business in a country with less strict securities laws than the CFA Institute's Code and Standards, the member must adhere to the

   A. Code and Standards
   B. Law of the less strict country
   C. Law of the country of residence

2. CFA charterholder Ponsart is hired by an investor-relations firm for a project to write a research paper on one of the firm's clients, a small software company. The firm will pay a flat fee plus a bonus if new investors buy stock in the company as a result of the report, and Ponsart accepts the payment arrangement. Did Ponsart any Standards of Professional Conduct?

   A. No
   B. Yes, relating to misrepresentation
   C. Yes, relating to independence and objectivity

3. CFA charterholder LeBlanc used recreational drugs on his lunch hour and returned to work where he made investment decisions for clients. Did LeBlanc violate any Standards of Professional Conduct?

   A. No
   B. Yes, relating to misconduct
   C. Yes, relating to duties to employers

4. Which statement is most accurate related to the Standard of Professional Conduct on material nonpublic information?

   A. Members and candidates must not engage in practices that distort prices or artificially inflate trading volume with the intent to mislead market participants
   B. Members and candidates must not knowingly make any misrepresentations relating to investment analysis, recommendations, actions, or other professional activities
   C. Members and candidates who possess material nonpublic information that could affect the value of an investment must not act or cause others to act on the information

Morning Exam

5. The owner of Chong Services agrees to promote the stock of companies in exchange for stock and compensation. The owner sends e-mails and newsletters and creates web sites containing inaccurate information to promote the stock which leads to higher stock prices. The owner violated the Standards of Professional Conduct relating to

    A. Independence and objectivity, market manipulation, and duties to clients
    B. Fair dealing, independence and objectivity, and additional compensation agreements
    C. Market manipulation, diligence and reasonable basis, and disclosure of conflicts

6. CFA charterholder Tilak sends an e-mail to all his clients with a buy recommendation then calls his largest clients to discuss the recommendation. Did Tilak violate any Standards of Professional Conduct?

    A. No
    B. Yes, relating to fair dealing
    C. Yes, relating to market manipulation

7. CFA charterholder Gwyer is an asset manager for a pension fund and is advised that a client has probably violated tax and fiduciary regulations and laws related to a pension fund. What is Gwyer's most appropriate response after informing her supervisor if her employer is not successful in taking steps to have the client remedy the situation?

    A. Resign as asset manager
    B. Seek advice of legal counsel
    C. Disclose the evidence to government officials

8. CFA charterholder Mehta works for a firm as a research analyst, gets permission from his employer to run for mayor of his hometown, and is elected. Did Mehta violate any Standards of Professional Conduct?

    A. No
    B. Yes, relating to loyalty
    C. Yes, relating to disclosure of conflicts

9. CFA charterholder Yang supervises CFA charterholder Springer at a registered investment advisory and registered broker/dealer firm. Yang finds that Springer places a large number of trades of a thinly traded security at the end of each month and asks Springer about it, who replies that it was a client's request. Six months later, Springer is investigated for manipulating prices at month's end. Did Yang violate any Standards of Professional Conduct?

    A. No
    B. Yes, he failed to supervise adequately
    C. Yes, he failed to report the activity to authorities

Morning Exam

10. CFA charterholder Bergman is an aggressive growth manager that has invested in small caps since inception. Bergman changed its maximum capitalization from $250 million to $500 million, and prepared literature to inform prospective clients and third-party consultants of the change. Existing clients are not notified. Did Bergman violate any Standards of Professional Conduct?

    A. No
    B. Yes, relating to misrepresentation
    C. Yes, relating to communications with clients and prospective clients

11. CFA charterholder Hammond founded an investment club that has been inactive for a year. Hammond's employer requires disclosure of all stock ownership. Hammond did not disclose the investment club to his employer. Hammond most likely violated

    A. His employer's policies and the Standards of Professional Conduct
    B. His employer's policies but not the Standards of Professional Conduct
    C. The Standards of Professional Conduct but not his employer's policies

12. CFA charterholder Marmelo is a director at a bank and attended a board meeting at a company to discuss renegotiating the company's debt. Marmelo puts in a sell order for all of his shares of the company before the meeting. Which Standard of Professional Conduct did Marmelo least likely violate?

    A. Misrepresentation
    B. Material nonpublic information
    C. Disclosure of conflicts of interest

13. Which is an improper reference to the CFA Institute, the CFA designation, or the CFA program?

    A. CFA, Level II
    B. The CFA designation is globally recognized
    C. Passed all 3 CFA exams in 3 consecutive years

14. CFA charterholder Whitehurst provides investment advice to a private endowment. The trustees have provided Whitehurst with comprehensive financial information. A prominent alumnus, Murdoch, calls Whitehurst to request comprehensive financial information about the fund because he has a potential contributor but needs the information to close the deal and he cannot contact any of the trustees. Whitehurst's best course of action is to

    A. Not send the information to preserve confidentiality
    B. Send the information because the disclosure would benefit the client
    C. Send the information because it is not material nonpublic information

Morning Exam

15. CFA charterholder Shahperi works for an investment counseling firm. Sopko, a new client, meets Shahperi for the first time. After introducing themselves, before asking about investment objectives, Shahperi immediately explains to Sopko that she has found an undervalued stock and she recommends that Sopko buy it. Which Standard of Professional Conduct did Shahperi most likely violate?

    A. Suitability
    B. Fair dealing
    C. Priority of transactions

16. CFA charterholder Ramthun submits his resignation. After work prior, to his last day of employment, he makes preparations to start his own firm. After his last day, he contacts friends who were former clients to solicit their business. Did Ramthun violate any Standards of Professional Conduct?

    A. No
    B. Yes, by soliciting clients of his former employer
    C. Yes, by using privileged information the belongs to his employer

17. What is critical to effective compliance with the GIPS standards?

    A. Verification
    B. Consistency of input data
    C. Centralized global regulation

18. Which section of the GIPS incorporates the information from the input data, calculating returns, constructing the composites, and disclosures?

    A. Recommendations
    B. Presentation and reporting
    C. Fundamentals of compliance

19. What is the value of a $100,000 deposit after two years of earning 4% compounded continuously?

    A. $108,000
    B. $108,286
    C. $108,329

Morning Exam

20. Should a firm accept or reject an investment costing $3.35 million that is expected to increase annual cash flows by $1 million for each of the next five years, using a cost of capital of 12%?

    A. Reject
    B. It depends on whether NPV or IRR is used
    C. Accept

21. What measurement scale would be used for credit ratings for bond issues?

    A. Ordinal scale
    B. Ratio scale
    C. Nominal scale

22. What is the median and mode of the credit ratings Aaa, Aa3, A2, A2, Baa1, B1, Caa, Ca, and C?

    A. Median = Baa1, mode = A2
    B. Median = A2, mode = A2
    C. Median = A2, mode = Baa1

23. Using Chebyshev's inequality, what is the range that must contain at least 75% of observations with a mean of 9% and a standard deviation of 5%?

    A. 4% to 14%
    B. -1% to 19%
    C. -6% to 24%

24. What is a characteristic of a normal distribution?

    A. Skewed
    B. Symmetric
    C. The mean is less than the median

25. If stocks have positive returns 75% of the time, bonds have positive returns 80% of the time, and both have positive returns 60% of the time, what is the probability that both asset classes are negative or zero?

    A. 5%
    B. 10%
    C. 20%

Morning Exam

26. What is the covariance of returns if when the return on one asset is above or below its expected value, the return on the other asset is in the opposite direction relative to its expected value?

    A. Negative
    B. Zero
    C. Positive

27. Given that P(X<=1)=0.10, P(X<=2)=0.50, P(X<=3)=0.70, and P(X<=4)=1.00, what is p(1)?

    A. 0.0
    B. 0.1
    C. 0.4

28. If a manager can be expected to keep within a tracking error of 75 basis points 90% of the time, what is the probability that a manager has a tracking error outside 75 basis points three years in a row?

    A. 0.1%
    B. 2.7%
    C. 2.8%

29. Approximately what percent of normally distributed portfolios with a mean return of 10% and a standard deviation of 12% have a return that exceeds the risk-free rate of 4%?

    A. 68%
    B. 75%
    C. 84%

30. Which is closest to the probability that the return on the optimal portfolio will be less than the threshold level when a client with a portfolio of $100,000 would like to withdraw $5,000 at the year end and avoid the balance dropping below $100,000: allocation 1 with an expected return of 10% and a standard deviation of 20%, allocation 2 with an expected return of 11% and a standard deviation of 30%, or allocation 3 with an expected return of 8% and a standard deviation of 10%, given that P(Z<=0.00) = 0.5000; P(Z<=0.25) = 0.5987; P(Z<=0.50) = 0.6915; P(Z<=0.75) = 0.7734; and P(Z<=1.00) = 0.8413?

    A. 24%
    B. 38%
    C. 76%

Morning Exam

31. What is the approximate reliability factor for a 90% confidence interval?

    A. 1.65
    B. 1.96
    C. 2.58

32. What sampling issue comes from finding models by repeatedly searching through databases for patterns until finding something that appears to work?

    A. Data-mining bias
    B. Sample selection bias
    C. Survivorship bias

33. What happens to total revenue after a price cut if demand is elastic?

    A. Increases
    B. Decreases
    C. Stays the same

34. What best describes pollution?

    A. Externality
    B. Free-rider problem
    C. Transaction cost

35. Which is least likely to be considered a disadvantage of a proprietorship or partnership?

    A. High cost of capital and labor
    B. Owner's or owners' entire wealth at risk
    C. Retained profits taxed twice

36. What is least likely to happen with an increase in the price of a factor of production such as rent or other component of fixed costs?

    A. Shifts the total cost curve downward
    B. Leaves the variable cost curves and the marginal cost curves unchanged
    C. Shifts the fixed cost curves upward

37. What is the shape of the long-run cost curve with diseconomies of scale?

    A. Downward sloping
    B. U-shaped
    C. Upward sloping

Morning Exam

38. What is the change in total revenue that results from a one-unit increase in the quantity sold?

    A. Marginal revenue
    B. Marginal revenue product
    C. Derived demand

39. What is the supply of a factor when its entire income is made up of opportunity cost?

    A. Perfectly inelastic
    B. Perfectly elastic
    C. Elastic

40. Which is most likely to increase potential GDP?

    A. The quantity of capital increases
    B. The full-employment quantity of labor decreases
    C. The money wage rate rises

41. Banks devising new types of deposits on which checks could be written is an example of what?

    A. Regulation to restrict innovation
    B. Deregulation in response to innovation
    C. Innovation to avoid regulation

42. What is least likely to trigger demand-pull inflation?

    A. Decrease in money wage rate
    B. Cut in the interest rate
    C. Increase in the quantity of money

43. Which is least likely to be considered directly responsible for the conduct of monetary policy?

    A. Federal Open Market Committee (FOMC)
    B. Board of Governors of the Federal Reserve System
    C. Congress

44. Which is least likely to result from the Federal Reserve System buying securities in the open market?

    A. Fed assets increase
    B. Fed liabilities decrease
    C. Creates bank reserves

Morning Exam

45. What equals revenue minus expenses?

    A. Income
    B. Cash flow
    C. Owners' equity

46. What is owners' equity?

    A. Liabilities minus assets
    B. Revenue minus expenses
    C. Contributed capital plus retained earnings

47. What entry is made to reduce a liability as an accrued expense is paid?

    A. Adjusting entry
    B. Originating entry
    C. No accrual entry needed

48. Which is least likely to contribute to the qualitative characteristic of reliability?

    A. Accuracy
    B. Substance over form
    C. Faithful representation

49. Which is a characteristic of an effective financial reporting framework?

    A. Accuracy
    B. Rules based
    C. Transparency

50. What is an income statement without a subtotal for gross profit?

    A. Multi-step format
    B. Single-step format
    C. Grouping by nature

51. Which is closest to the revenue that will be reported in the third year under the percentage-of-completion method if the costs incurred and paid are $0.6 million the first year, $3.0 million the second year, and $0.8 million the third year; and the amounts billed and received are $1.2 million the first year, $2.8 million the second year, and $1.3 million the third year?

    A. $0.7 million
    B. $0.8 million
    C. $1.0 million

Morning Exam

52. Which would be least likely to require an estimate for expense recognition?

    A. Cost of sales
    B. Warranty expenses
    C. Uncollectible accounts

53. How is diluted EPS calculated for convertible securities?

    A. The same as basic EPS
    B. The treasury stock method
    C. The if-converted method

54. What type of balance sheet lists assets, liabilities, and equity in a single column?

    A. Report format
    B. Account format
    C. Ledger account

55. Repurchasing stock would be in what category on a cash flow statement?

    A. Investing
    B. Operating
    C. Financing

56. What category on a cash flow statement includes day-to-day activities?

    A. Operating
    B. Financing
    C. Investing

57. Which is the most likely cause of a substantial drop in cash flow from operations?

    A. Decrease in receivables
    B. Increase in inventory
    C. Increase in proportion of cash sales

58. If a company wrote down inventory by $100,000 from $500,000 due to an oversupply, and the next year prices increased 10%, what will inventory most likely be reported at under IFRS?

    A. $400,000
    B. $500,000
    C. $550,000

Morning Exam

59. In a period of rising prices, which is most likely greater for a company that uses LIFO compared to a company that uses FIFO?

    A. Net income
    B. Cost of sales
    C. Income taxes

60. What would most likely be decreased in the early periods of an asset's life for a company uses accelerated depreciation rather than straight-line depreciation?

    A. Asset turnover ratios
    B. Shareholders' equity
    C. Cash flow from operations

61. If company A has equipment that cost $6 million, accumulated depreciation of $4 million, and annual depreciation expense of $1 million; company B has equipment that cost $16 million, accumulated depreciation of $10 million, and annual depreciation expense of $2 million; and company C has equipment that cost $21 million, accumulated depreciation of $9 million, and annual depreciation expense of $3 million; which company's equipment has the highest average age?

    A. Company A
    B. Company B
    C. Company C

62. What is the tax base of a liability with respect to revenue received in advance?

    A. The carrying amount less any amount of revenue that will be taxable in future
    B. The carrying amount less any amount of revenue that will not be taxable in future
    C. Any amount of revenue that will be taxable in the future less the carrying amount

63. Which records an offsetting credit in income for previously unrecognized tax losses of the acquirer?

    A. U.S. GAAP but not IFRS
    B. IFRS but not U.S. GAAP
    C. Both U.S. GAAP and IFRS

Morning Exam

64. For a capital lease with rental payments of $5,000 per year, fair value of leased equipment at inception of $30,000, an implicit interest rate of 10%, with the present value of the lease equal to the present value of the equipment at inception, which is closest to the interest recorded by the lessee in the second year of the lease?

    A. $2,700
    B. $2,800
    C. $3,000

65. What kind of ratios measure the ability of a company to meet short-term obligations?

    A. Activity ratios
    B. Liquidity ratios
    C. Solvency ratios

66. Calculate return on equity (ROE) if sales divided by total assets are 3, net profit margin is 4%, return on total assets is 12%, and total assets divided by equity is 1.6?

    A. 2.3%
    B. 6.4%
    C. 19.2%

67. How are inventory write-downs treated under IASB standards?

    A. Not allowed
    B. Allowed but not reversible
    C. Allowed and subject to reversal

68. What would an analyst recalculate to eliminate the effect of write-ups when comparing an IFRS company that has written up the value of intangible assets to a U.S. company?

    A. Gross margin
    B. Earnings per share
    C. Any affected asset-based ratios

69. Which category of projects susceptible to the capital budgeting process is most likely to generate no revenue and have a negative present value?

    A. Replacement
    B. Regulatory, safety, and environmental
    C. Expansion and new products and services

Morning Exam

70. What is the discounted payback period closest to if the initial investment is $40 million, the cash flows are $15 million per year at the end of the each of 4 years, and the required rate of return is 10%?

    A. 0.13 years longer than the payback method
    B. 0.26 years longer than the payback method
    C. 0.59 years longer than the payback method

71. Which is preferred if a company must choose one project between two mutually exclusive projects; project A with an NPV of $60 million and an IRR of 15%; and project B with an NPV of $50 million and an IRR of 20%?

    A. Project A because it has a greater NPV
    B. Project B because it has a greater IRR
    C. Project B because it has a lower NPV

72. What is the weighted average cost of capital (WACC) for a company with a capital structure of 30% debt, 10% preferred stock, and 60% equity; a before-tax cost of debt of 9%; cost of preferred stock of 12%; cost of equity of 14%; and a 40% tax rate?

    A. 10.74%
    B. 11.22%
    C. 12.30%

73. What is an estimate of the cost of retained earnings using the capital asset pricing model (CAPM) approach if the current dividends are $1, the market price is $20, ROE is 12%, the dividend payout rate is 20%, the risk-free rate is 4%, beta is 1.3, and the expected return on the market portfolio is 13%?

    A. 15.1%
    B. 15.7%
    C. 17.2%

74. Which is closest to the weighted average cost of capital (WACC) if the average unlevered beta for comparable companies is 0.8, the tax rate is 20%, the target debt-to-equity ratio is 0.25, the risk-free rate is 3%, the equity risk premium is 6%, and the cost of debt is 300 basis points over the risk-free rate?

    A. 7.97%
    B. 8.21%
    C. 8.76%

Morning Exam

75. Which is least likely to indicate greater liquidity?

    A. Greater quick ratio
    B. Greater current ratio
    C. Greater number of days of receivables

76. Which is closest to the cost of trade credit if the terms are 1/10, net 30, and the account is paid on the 30th day?

    A. 13%
    B. 20%
    C. 44%

77. Which is closest to the tax effect if the operating profit margin is 7.7%, the effect on non-operating items is 0.9, total asset turnover is 1.5, financial leverage is 1.2, and the return on equity is 10%?

    A. 0.6
    B. 0.7
    C. 0.8

78. Which is good corporate governance for voting?

    A. Votes are counted by a third party
    B. Shareowners must be present to vote
    C. Only management votes for corporate changes

79. External or informational efficiency means

    A. Low transaction costs
    B. Prices do not change rapidly
    C. Market prices reflect all available information

80. The minimum pretax income included as a listing requirement for the NYSE in 2004 was $2.5

    A. Million for the last year and $2.0 million for the last two years
    B. Billion last year and $2.0 billion for the last two years
    C. Trillion last year and $2.0 trillion for the last two years

81. Short sellers

    A. Lend securities
    B. Borrow securities
    C. Place limit orders

Morning Exam

82. For a margin account with an initial deposit of $5,000 used to purchase 200 shares of stock at $50, and a maintenance margin of 25%, what is the margin call closest to if the stock declines to $30?

    A. $0
    B. $500
    C. $1,000

83. What is closest to the return on the value weighted index for three stocks with prices at the beginning of the year for stocks A, B, and C of $11, $20, and $17, respectively, prices at the end of the year for stocks A, B, and C of $14, $25, and $15, respectively, and 3 million shares of stock A, 20 million shares of stock B, and 6 million shares of stock C?

    A. 12.0%
    B. 13.5%
    C. 18.1%

84. Which form of the efficient market hypothesis (EMH) is tested by time-series analysis, cross-sectional analysis, or event studies?

    A. Weak form
    B. Strong form
    C. Semi-strong form

85. Which is least likely to be considered a problem that may prevent arbitrageurs from correcting anomalies?

    A. It is unclear when mispricing will disappear
    B. Arbitrageurs have an unlimited amount of capital
    C. It is rare to find two assets with exactly the same risk

86. Which is least likely to explain why valid anomalies may not be profitable?

    A. Conditions governing anomalies are constant
    B. Documented anomalies are based on averages
    C. Positive abnormal returns do not mean positive returns

87. Which is closest to the P/E ratio of a common stock with a dividend payout ratio of 50%, a dividend growth rate of 7%, and a required rate of return of 11%?

    A. 12.50 = 50% / (11% - 7%)
    B. 13.38
    C. 13.88

Morning Exam

88. Which is closest to price of a share using the dividend discount model (DDM) with a dividend payout ratio of 60%, a dividend growth rate of 5.1%, a required rate of return of 12.6%, a weighted-average cost of capital of 12%, and current earnings per share of $2?

    A. $16.00
    B. $16.82
    C. $18.28

89. What is the estimated price of a stock using the dividend discount model if the earnings retention ratio is 50%, the ROE is 20%, the current dividends are $2 per share, and the required rate of return is 15%?

    A. $44
    B. $45
    C. $50

90. Which is least likely to be considered a rationale for using price to sales value (P / S) ratios?

    A. Reflects a company's expenses
    B. Sales are positive even when EPS is negative
    C. Less subject to manipulation than EPS or book value

91. Which is least likely to be a forward commitment for all parties involved?

    A. Swap
    B. Put option
    C. Futures contract

92. What is a commitment for one party, the long, to buy a currency at a fixed price from the other party, the short?

    A. Eurodollar time deposit
    B. Currency forward contract
    C. Forward rate agreement (FRA)

Morning Exam

93. What is the ending balance at the end of day 4 for a holder of a short position of 20 futures contracts if the initial futures price on day 0 is $212, the initial margin requirement is $10, the maintenance margin requirement is $7.50, the settlement price on day 1 is $211, the settlement price on day 2 is $214, the settlement price on day 3 is $209, and the settlement price on day 4 is $210?

   A. $160
   B. $220
   C. $240

94. An investor buys a call at $95 for $2 when the price of the stock was $95. What is the intrinsic value of the call if the new price of the stock is $94?

   A. -$1.00
   B. $0.00
   C. $1.00

95. An asset manager enters into a $25 million equity swap and agrees to pay a dealer a fixed rate of 4.5% and the dealer agrees to pay the return on a large-cap index. Payments are made semi-annually based on 180 days out of a 365-day year. The value of the large-cap index starts at 578.50. In six months, the small cap index is at 581.35. Which party pays what amount after the payments are netted?

   A. The dealer pays the asset manager $677,958
   B. The asset manager pays the dealer $431,632
   C. The asset manager pays the dealer $677,958

96. What is the maximum loss for a covered call option at expiration, for a stock selling for $98 and a call option at $105 selling for $8?

   A. $90
   B. $98
   C. Unlimited

97. What sets forth a formula for calculating the amount the issue must pay to call an issue to protect the yield of investors?

   A. Deferred call
   B. Call schedule
   C. Make-whole premium

Morning Exam

98. What is the price of a bond when the coupon rate is equal to the yield required by the market?

    A. Equal to par value
    B. Less than par value
    C. Greater then par value

99. What is a security's price sensitivity to changes in yield?

    A. Duration
    B. Convexity
    C. Dollar duration

100. Which feature is least likely to increase reinvestment risk?

    A. Callable
    B. Amortizing
    C. Zero-coupon

101. A decrease in expected yield volatility will cause the value of

    A. Callable bonds to decrease
    B. Putable bonds to increase
    C. Putable bonds to decrease

102. An investor purchases $10,000 of par value of a Treasury inflation protection security (TIPS). The real rate determined at the auction is 3.8%. If at the end of the first six months the CPI-U is 2.4% on an annual rate and at the end of the second six months the CPI-U is 2.8% on an annual basis, which is closest to the coupon payment at the end of the second six months?

    A. $192.28
    B. $194.97
    C. $261.68

103. What are the most common internal credit enhancements for asset-backed securities?

    A. Reserve funds, letter of credit, and bond insurance
    B. Corporate guarantee, letter of credit, and bond insurance
    C. Reserve funds, over collateralization, and senior/subordinate structures

Morning Exam

104. What is the relative yield spread between a 5-year bond with a 5.11% yield and a 5-year on-the-run Treasury with a 4.18% yield?

    A. 93 basis points
    B. 22.2%
    C. 1.222

105. As a bond moves closer to maturity, assuming the discount rate does not change, a bond's value

    A. Increases over time if the bond is selling at a premium
    B. Increases over time if the bond is selling at a discount
    C. Decreases over time if the bond is selling at par

106. At what interest rate do bond cash flows need to be reinvested for an investment to achieve the yield to maturity?

    A. Current yield
    B. Yield to maturity
    C. Bond-equivalent yield

107. Which is closest to the value of a $100 par, 1.5-year, 6% coupon Treasury bond if the forward rates for the periods 1, 2, and 3 are 3.00%, 3.60%, and 3.92%, respectively?

    A. $96
    B. $102
    C. $104

108. What is a measure of the approximate percentage change in price for a 100 basis point change in rates?

    A. Duration
    B. Convexity
    C. Price value of a basis point (PVBP)

109. Which is closest to the duration of a portfolio with $200,000 in a bond with a duration of 4; $300,000 in a bond with a duration of 6; $250,000 in a bond with a duration of 7; and $550,000 in a bond with a duration of 8?

    A. 6.73
    B. 7.06
    C. 7.73

Morning Exam

110. Which is closest to percentage price change for a 5% 25-year bond with duration of 14.19 and convexity of 141.68 if yields decrease by 200 basis points?

    A. 22.71%
    B. 28.38%
    C. 34.05%

111. What is fee simple real estate?

    A. Mortgaged
    B. Leveraged equity
    C. Free and clear equity

112. A real estate investment project had a purchase price of $700,000 which is financed 20% by equity and is sold at the end of five years. Which is closest to the internal rate of return (IRR) of the project if the property has after-tax cash flow for the first five years of $21,575, $24,361, $27,280, $30,339, and $273,629, and the present value of after tax cash flows is $164,012 at 22%, $144,303 at 26%, and $127,747 at 30%?

    A. 27%
    B. 28%
    C. 29%

113. Which is closest to the probability of survival through the end of seven years for a project with a failure probability in year 1 of 0.25, in year 2 of 0.22, and in each of years 3 through 7 of 0.20?

    A. 0.0%
    B. 19.2%
    C. 80.8%

114. Which statement is least accurate regarding hedge funds?

    A. A hedge fund searches for absolute returns
    B. A hedge fund is an actively managed investment vehicle using a variety of strategies
    C. All hedge funds offer plays against the market by using short selling, futures, and derivatives

Morning Exam

115. Which is the first step in the portfolio management process, before the investment strategy?

    A. Policy statement
    B. Continual monitoring
    C. Construct the portfolio

116. From 1934 through 2003, during what percentage of one-year holding periods did stock returns trail T-bill returns?

    A. 11.5%
    B. 35.7%
    C. 64.3%

117. If an investor has a portfolio with equal weights of four securities with returns of 10%, 12%, 16%, and 22%, what will happen to the expected return for the portfolio if the security with the 16% return is replaced with a security with a return equal to the original portfolio?

    A. Increases
    B. Decreases
    C. Remains the same

118. Which is closest to the standard deviation of a portfolio with a 50% weight in each of two securities, both of which have an expected return of 20% and a standard deviation of 10%, if the correlation coefficient is -0.5?

    A. 5%
    B. 7%
    C. 9%

119. Which is least likely to be considered an assumption of capital market theory?

    A. Investors target points on the efficient frontier
    B. Investors can borrow or lend money at the risk-free rate
    C. Investors estimate different probability distributions for future rates of return

120. Which is closest to the number of securities needed in a portfolio to approach 90% of the variance with complete diversification?

    A. 15 to 18
    B. 60 to 72
    C. 120 to 144

Morning Exam

1. A	41. C	81. B
2. C	42. A	82. B
3. B	43. C	83. C
4. C	44. B	84. C
5. C	45. A	85. B
6. A	46. C	86. A
7. B	47. A	87. A
8. A	48. A	88. B
9. B	49. C	89. A
10. C	50. B	90. A
11. A	51. C	91. B
12. A	52. A	92. B
13. A	53. C	93. C
14. A	54. A	94. B
15. A	55. C	95. B
16. A	56. A	96. A
17. B	57. B	97. C
18. B	58. B	98. A
19. C	59. B	99. A
20. C	60. B	100. C
21. A	61. B	101. C
22. A	62. B	102. B
23. B	63. B	103. C
24. B	64. B	104. B
25. B	65. B	105. B
26. A	66. C	106. B
27. B	67. C	107. C
28. A	68. C	108. A
29. B	69. B	109. A
30. B	70. C	110. C
31. A	71. A	111. C
32. A	72. B	112. A
33. A	73. B	113. B
34. A	74. A	114. C
35. C	75. C	115. A
36. A	76. B	116. B
37. C	77. C	117. B
38. A	78. A	118. A
39. B	79. C	119. C
40. A	80. A	120. A

Morning Exam

1. If a member resides in a country with no securities laws or regulations and does business in a country with less strict securities laws than the CFA Institute's Code and Standards, the member must adhere to the

   *A. Code and Standards (Standard I(A) - knowledge of the law)
   B. Law of the less strict country
   C. Law of the country of residence

2. CFA charterholder Ponsart is hired by an investor-relations firm for a project to write a research paper on one of the firm's clients, a small software company. The firm will pay a flat fee plus a bonus if new investors buy stock in the company as a result of the report, and Ponsart accepts the payment arrangement. Did Ponsart any Standards of Professional Conduct?

   A. No
   B. Yes, relating to misrepresentation
   *C. Yes, relating to independence and objectivity (Standard I(B) - independence and objectivity)

3. CFA charterholder LeBlanc used recreational drugs on his lunch hour and returned to work where he made investment decisions for clients. Did LeBlanc violate any Standards of Professional Conduct?

   A. No
   *B. Yes, relating to misconduct (Standard I(D) - misconduct)
   C. Yes, relating to duties to employers

4. Which statement is most accurate related to the Standard of Professional Conduct on material nonpublic information?

   A. Members and candidates must not engage in practices that distort prices or artificially inflate trading volume with the intent to mislead market participants
   B. Members and candidates must not knowingly make any misrepresentations relating to investment analysis, recommendations, actions, or other professional activities
   *C. Members and candidates who possess material nonpublic information that could affect the value of an investment must not act or cause others to act on the information

Morning Exam

5. The owner of Chong Services agrees to promote the stock of companies in exchange for stock and compensation. The owner sends e-mails and newsletters and creates web sites containing inaccurate information to promote the stock which leads to higher stock prices. The owner violated the Standards of Professional Conduct relating to

   A. Independence and objectivity, market manipulation, and duties to clients
   B. Fair dealing, independence and objectivity, and additional compensation agreements
   *C. Market manipulation, diligence and reasonable basis, and disclosure of conflicts (Standard II(B) - market manipulation, Standard V(A) - diligence and reasonable basis, and Standard VI(A) - disclosure of conflicts)

6. CFA charterholder Tilak sends an e-mail to all his clients with a buy recommendation then calls his largest clients to discuss the recommendation. Did Tilak violate any Standards of Professional Conduct?

   *A. No (Standard III(B) - fair dealing)
   B. Yes, relating to fair dealing
   C. Yes, relating to market manipulation

7. CFA charterholder Gwyer is an asset manager for a pension fund and is advised that a client has probably violated tax and fiduciary regulations and laws related to a pension fund. What is Gwyer's most appropriate response after informing her supervisor if her employer is not successful in taking steps to have the client remedy the situation?

   A. Resign as asset manager
   *B. Seek advice of legal counsel (Standard III(E) - preservation of confidentiality)
   C. Disclose the evidence to government officials

8. CFA charterholder Mehta works for a firm as a research analyst, gets permission from his employer to run for mayor of his hometown, and is elected. Did Mehta violate any Standards of Professional Conduct?

   *A. No (Standard IV(A) - loyalty)
   B. Yes, relating to loyalty
   C. Yes, relating to disclosure of conflicts

Morning Exam

9. CFA charterholder Yang supervises CFA charterholder Springer at a registered investment advisory and registered broker/dealer firm. Yang finds that Springer places a large number of trades of a thinly traded security at the end of each month and asks Springer about it, who replies that it was a client's request. Six months later, Springer is investigated for manipulating prices at month's end. Did Yang violate any Standards of Professional Conduct?

   A. No
   *B. Yes, he failed to supervise adequately (Standard IV(C) - responsibilities of supervisors)
   C. Yes, he failed to report the activity to authorities

10. CFA charterholder Bergman is an aggressive growth manager that has invested in small caps since inception. Bergman changed its maximum capitalization from $250 million to $500 million, and prepared literature to inform prospective clients and third-party consultants of the change. Existing clients are not notified. Did Bergman violate any Standards of Professional Conduct?

    A. No
    B. Yes, relating to misrepresentation
    *C. Yes, relating to communications with clients and prospective clients (Standard V(B) - communications with clients and prospective clients)

11. CFA charterholder Hammond founded an investment club that has been inactive for a year. Hammond's employer requires disclosure of all stock ownership. Hammond did not disclose the investment club to his employer. Hammond most likely violated

    *A. His employer's policies and the Standards of Professional Conduct (Standard VI(A) - disclosure of conflicts and Standard IV - duties to employers)
    B. His employer's policies but not the Standards of Professional Conduct
    C. The Standards of Professional Conduct but not his employer's policies

12. CFA charterholder Marmelo is a director at a bank and attended a board meeting at a company to discuss renegotiating the company's debt. Marmelo puts in a sell order for all of his shares of the company before the meeting. Which Standard of Professional Conduct did Marmelo least likely violate?

    *A. Misrepresentation (Standard VI(A) - disclosure of conflicts and Standard II(A) - material nonpublic information)
    B. Material nonpublic information
    C. Disclosure of conflicts of interest

Morning Exam

13. Which is an improper reference to the CFA Institute, the CFA designation, or the CFA program?

    *A. CFA, Level II (Standard VII(B) - reference to the CFA Institute, the CFA designation, and the CFA program)
    B. The CFA designation is globally recognized
    C. Passed all 3 CFA exams in 3 consecutive years

14. CFA charterholder Whitehurst provides investment advice to a private endowment. The trustees have provided Whitehurst with comprehensive financial information. A prominent alumnus, Murdoch, calls Whitehurst to request comprehensive financial information about the fund because he has a potential contributor but needs the information to close the deal and he cannot contact any of the trustees. Whitehurst's best course of action is to

    *A. Not send the information to preserve confidentiality (Standard III(D) - preservation of confidentiality)
    B. Send the information because the disclosure would benefit the client
    C. Send the information because it is not material nonpublic information

15. CFA charterholder Shahperi works for an investment counseling firm. Sopko, a new client, meets Shahperi for the first time. After introducing themselves, before asking about investment objectives, Shahperi immediately explains to Sopko that she has found an undervalued stock and she recommends that Sopko buy it. Which Standard of Professional Conduct did Shahperi most likely violate?

    *A. Suitability (Standard III(C) - suitability)
    B. Fair dealing
    C. Priority of transactions

16. CFA charterholder Ramthun submits his resignation. After work prior, to his last day of employment, he makes preparations to start his own firm. After his last day, he contacts friends who were former clients to solicit their business. Did Ramthun violate any Standards of Professional Conduct?

    *A. No (Standard IV(A) - loyalty)
    B. Yes, by soliciting clients of his former employer
    C. Yes, by using privileged information the belongs to his employer

17. What is critical to effective compliance with the GIPS standards?

    A. Verification
    *B. Consistency of input data
    C. Centralized global regulation

Morning Exam

18. Which section of the GIPS incorporates the information from the input data, calculating returns, constructing the composites, and disclosures?

    A. Recommendations
    *B. Presentation and reporting
    C. Fundamentals of compliance

19. What is the value of a $100,000 deposit after two years of earning 4% compounded continuously?

    A. $108,000
    B. $108,286
    *C. $108,329 = $100,000 (e^((.04)(2))); continuous compounding can be approximated using 1,000 compounding periods per year; n = 2,000, i = 0.004, PV = -100,000, PMT = 0; FV = $108,329

20. Should a firm accept or reject an investment costing $3.35 million that is expected to increase annual cash flows by $1 million for each of the next five years, using a cost of capital of 12%?

    A. Reject
    B. It depends on whether NPV or IRR is used
    *C. Accept; because NPV = $0.255 million and IRR = 15%; 3.605 = [(1 - (1/1.12)^5] / .12 and 3.350 = [(1 - (1/1.15)^5] / .15; 3.605 - 3.350 = 0.255; NPV: n = 5, i = 12%, PMT = 1,000,000, FV = 0; PV = $3,604,776; $3,604,776 - $3,335,000 = $254,776 = $0.255 million; IRR: n = 5, PV = -3,350,000, PMT = 1,000,000, FV = 0; i = 15.03 percent = 15.03%

21. What measurement scale would be used for credit ratings for bond issues?

    *A. Ordinal scale
    B. Ratio scale
    C. Nominal scale

22. What is the median and mode of the credit ratings Aaa, Aa3, A2, A2, Baa1, B1, Caa, Ca, and C?

    *A. Median = Baa1, mode = A2
    B. Median = A2, mode = A2
    C. Median = A2, mode = Baa1

Morning Exam

23. Using Chebyshev's inequality, what is the range that must contain at least 75% of observations with a mean of 9% and a standard deviation of 5%?

    A. 4% to 14%
    *B. -1% to 19%; or 9% +/- 2(5%)
    C. -6% to 24%

24. What is a characteristic of a normal distribution?

    A. Skewed
    *B. Symmetric
    C. The mean is less than the median

25. If stocks have positive returns 75% of the time, bonds have positive returns 80% of the time, and both have positive returns 60% of the time, what is the probability that both asset classes are negative or zero?

    A. 5%
    *B. 10% = 100% - (80% + 75% - 65%)
    C. 20%

26. What is the covariance of returns if when the return on one asset is above or below its expected value, the return on the other asset is in the opposite direction relative to its expected value?

    *A. Negative
    B. Zero
    C. Positive

27. Given that $P(X<=1)=0.10$, $P(X<=2)=0.50$, $P(X<=3)=0.70$, and $P(X<=4)=1.00$, what is $p(1)$?

    A. 0.0
    *B. 0.1
    C. 0.4

28. If a manager can be expected to keep within a tracking error of 75 basis points 90% of the time, what is the probability that a manager has a tracking error outside 75 basis points three years in a row?

    *A. 0.1% = .1^3
    B. 2.7%
    C. 2.8%

Morning Exam

29. Approximately what percent of normally distributed portfolios with a mean return of 10% and a standard deviation of 12% have a return that exceeds the risk-free rate of 4%?

   A. 68%
   *B. 75% = 1 - (1 - 50%)/2
   C. 84%

30. Which is closest to the probability that the return on the optimal portfolio will be less than the threshold level when a client with a portfolio of $100,000 would like to withdraw $5,000 at the year end and avoid the balance dropping below $100,000: allocation 1 with an expected return of 10% and a standard deviation of 20%, allocation 2 with an expected return of 11% and a standard deviation of 30%, or allocation 3 with an expected return of 8% and a standard deviation of 10%, given that P(Z<=0.00) = 0.5000; P(Z<=0.25) = 0.5987; P(Z<=0.50) = 0.6915; P(Z<=0.75) = 0.7734; and P(Z<=1.00) = 0.8413?

   A. 24%
   B. 38% = P{Z<= [-1((8%-5%)/10%)]} = 1 - P(Z<=0.30) = 1 - 0.6179; 24% would be closer for 1 - P(Z<=0.70) which is 1- 0.7580; 76% would be closer for 1 - P(Z<=-0.70), which is 1 - 0.2420
   C. 76%

31. What is the approximate reliability factor for a 90% confidence interval?

   *A. 1.65
   B. 1.96
   C. 2.58

32. What sampling issue comes from finding models by repeatedly searching through databases for patterns until finding something that appears to work?

   *A. Data-mining bias
   B. Sample selection bias
   C. Survivorship bias

33. What happens to total revenue after a price cut if demand is elastic?

   *A. Increases
   B. Decreases
   C. Stays the same

Morning Exam

34. What best describes pollution?

    *A. Externality
    B. Free-rider problem
    C. Transaction cost

35. Which is least likely to be considered a disadvantage of a proprietorship or partnership?

    A. High cost of capital and labor
    B. Owner's or owners' entire wealth at risk
    *C. Retained profits taxed twice

36. What is least likely to happen with an increase in the price of a factor of production such as rent or other component of fixed costs?

    *A. Shifts the total cost curve downward
    B. Leaves the variable cost curves and the marginal cost curves unchanged
    C. Shifts the fixed cost curves upward

37. What is the shape of the long-run cost curve with diseconomies of scale?

    A. Downward sloping
    B. U-shaped
    *C. Upward sloping

38. What is the change in total revenue that results from a one-unit increase in the quantity sold?

    *A. Marginal revenue
    B. Marginal revenue product
    C. Derived demand

39. What is the supply of a factor when its entire income is made up of opportunity cost?

    A. Perfectly inelastic
    *B. Perfectly elastic
    C. Elastic

40. Which is most likely to increase potential GDP?

    *A. The quantity of capital increases
    B. The full-employment quantity of labor decreases
    C. The money wage rate rises

Morning Exam

41. Banks devising new types of deposits on which checks could be written is an example of what?

    A. Regulation to restrict innovation
    B. Deregulation in response to innovation
    *C. Innovation to avoid regulation

42. What is least likely to trigger demand-pull inflation?

    *A. Decrease in money wage rate
    B. Cut in the interest rate
    C. Increase in the quantity of money

43. Which is least likely to be considered directly responsible for the conduct of monetary policy?

    A. Federal Open Market Committee (FOMC)
    B. Board of Governors of the Federal Reserve System
    *C. Congress

44. Which is least likely to result from the Federal Reserve System buying securities in the open market?

    A. Fed assets increase
    *B. Fed liabilities decrease
    C. Creates bank reserves

45. What equals revenue minus expenses?

    *A. Income
    B. Cash flow
    C. Owners' equity

46. What is owners' equity?

    A. Liabilities minus assets
    B. Revenue minus expenses
    *C. Contributed capital plus retained earnings

47. What entry is made to reduce a liability as an accrued expense is paid?

    *A. Adjusting entry
    B. Originating entry
    C. No accrual entry needed

Morning Exam

48. Which is least likely to contribute to the qualitative characteristic of reliability?

   *A. Accuracy
   B. Substance over form
   C. Faithful representation

49. Which is a characteristic of an effective financial reporting framework?

   A. Accuracy
   B. Rules based
   *C. Transparency

50. What is an income statement without a subtotal for gross profit?

   A. Multi-step format
   *B. Single-step format
   C. Grouping by nature

51. Which is closest to the revenue that will be reported in the third year under the percentage-of-completion method if the costs incurred and paid are $0.6 million the first year, $3.0 million the second year, and $0.8 million the third year; and the amounts billed and received are $1.2 million the first year, $2.8 million the second year, and $1.3 million the third year?

   A. $0.7 million
   B. $0.8 million
   *C. $1.0 million = ($0.8/$4.4) $5.3 million

52. Which would be least likely to require an estimate for expense recognition?

   *A. Cost of sales
   B. Warranty expenses
   C. Uncollectible accounts

53. How is diluted EPS calculated for convertible securities?

   A. The same as basic EPS
   B. The treasury stock method
   *C. The if-converted method

54. What type of balance sheet lists assets, liabilities, and equity in a single column?

   *A. Report format
   B. Account format
   C. Ledger account

Morning Exam

55. Repurchasing stock would be in what category on a cash flow statement?

    A. Investing
    B. Operating
    *C. Financing

56. What category on a cash flow statement includes day-to-day activities?

    *A. Operating
    B. Financing
    C. Investing

57. Which is the most likely cause of a substantial drop in cash flow from operations?

    A. Decrease in receivables
    *B. Increase in inventory
    C. Increase in proportion of cash sales

58. If a company wrote down inventory by $100,000 from $500,000 due to an oversupply, and the next year prices increased 10%, what will inventory most likely be reported at under IFRS?

    A. $400,000
    *B. $500,000
    C. $550,000

59. In a period of rising prices, which is most likely greater for a company that uses LIFO compared to a company that uses FIFO?

    A. Net income
    *B. Cost of sales
    C. Income taxes

60. What would most likely be decreased in the early periods of an asset's life for a company uses accelerated depreciation rather than straight-line depreciation?

    A. Asset turnover ratios
    *B. Shareholders' equity
    C. Cash flow from operations

Morning Exam

61. If company A has equipment that cost $6 million, accumulated depreciation of $4 million, and annual depreciation expense of $1 million; company B has equipment that cost $16 million, accumulated depreciation of $10 million, and annual depreciation expense of $2 million; and company C has equipment that cost $21 million, accumulated depreciation of $9 million, and annual depreciation expense of $3 million; which company's equipment has the highest average age?

   A. Company A
   *B. Company B; $10/$2 > $4/$1 > $9/$3
   C. Company C

62. What is the tax base of a liability with respect to revenue received in advance?

   A. The carrying amount less any amount of revenue that will be taxable in future
   *B. The carrying amount less any amount of revenue that will not be taxable in future
   C. Any amount of revenue that will be taxable in the future less the carrying amount

63. Which records an offsetting credit in income for previously unrecognized tax losses of the acquirer?

   A. U.S. GAAP but not IFRS
   *B. IFRS but not U.S. GAAP
   C. Both U.S. GAAP and IFRS

64. For a capital lease with rental payments of $5,000 per year, fair value of leased equipment at inception of $30,000, an implicit interest rate of 10%, with the present value of the lease equal to the present value of the equipment at inception, which is closest to the interest recorded by the lessee in the second year of the lease?

   A. $2,700
   *B. $2,800 = 10% [$30,000 - ($5,000 - 10%($30,000))]
   C. $3,000

65. What kind of ratios measure the ability of a company to meet short-term obligations?

   A. Activity ratios
   *B. Liquidity ratios
   C. Solvency ratios

66. Calculate return on equity (ROE) if sales divided by total assets are 3, net profit margin is 4%, return on total assets is 12%, and total assets divided by equity is 1.6?

   A. 2.3%
   B. 6.4%
   *C. 19.2% = 4%(3)(1.6)= 12%(1.6)

Morning Exam

67. How are inventory write-downs treated under IASB standards?

   A. Not allowed
   B. Allowed but not reversible
   *C. Allowed and subject to reversal

68. What would an analyst recalculate to eliminate the effect of write-ups when comparing an IFRS company that has written up the value of intangible assets to a U.S. company?

   A. Gross margin
   B. Earnings per share
   *C. Any affected asset-based ratios

69. Which category of projects susceptible to the capital budgeting process is most likely to generate no revenue and have a negative present value?

   A. Replacement
   *B. Regulatory, safety, and environmental
   C. Expansion and new products and services

70. What is the discounted payback period closest to if the initial investment is $40 million, the cash flows are $15 million per year at the end of the each of 4 years, and the required rate of return is 10%?

   A. 0.13 years longer than the payback method
   B. 0.26 years longer than the payback method
   *C. 0.59 years longer than the payback method = 3 + ($40 - $13.63 - $12.40 -$11.27) / $10.25 - $40 / $15

71. Which is preferred if a company must choose one project between two mutually exclusive projects; project A with an NPV of $60 million and an IRR of 15%; and project B with an NPV of $50 million and an IRR of 20%?

   *A. Project A because it has a greater NPV
   B. Project B because it has a greater IRR
   C. Project B because it has a lower NPV

72. What is the weighted average cost of capital (WACC) for a company with a capital structure of 30% debt, 10% preferred stock, and 60% equity; a before-tax cost of debt of 9%; cost of preferred stock of 12%; cost of equity of 14%; and a 40% tax rate?

   A. 10.74%
   *B. 11.22% = .3(9%)(1-.4) + .1(12%) + .6(14%)
   C. 12.30%

Morning Exam

73. What is an estimate of the cost of retained earnings using the capital asset pricing model (CAPM) approach if the current dividends are $1, the market price is $20, ROE is 12%, the dividend payout rate is 20%, the risk-free rate is 4%, beta is 1.3, and the expected return on the market portfolio is 13%?

    A. 15.1%
    *B. 15.7% = 4% + 1.3(13%-4%)
    C. 17.2%

74. Which is closest to the weighted average cost of capital (WACC) if the average unlevered beta for comparable companies is 0.8, the tax rate is 20%, the target debt-to-equity ratio is 0.25, the risk-free rate is 3%, the equity risk premium is 6%, and the cost of debt is 300 basis points over the risk-free rate?

    *A. 7.97% = [(.25/1.25)(3%+3%)(1-20%)] + [(1-.25/1.25){ 3% + (0.8)[1+(1-20%)0.25] 6%}]
    B. 8.21%
    C. 8.76%

75. Which is least likely to indicate greater liquidity?

    A. Greater quick ratio
    B. Greater current ratio
    *C. Greater number of days of receivables

76. Which is closest to the cost of trade credit if the terms are 1/10, net 30, and the account is paid on the 30th day?

    A. 13%
    *B. 20% = [1 + .01/(1-.01)]^(365/20) - 1
    C. 44%

77. Which is closest to the tax effect if the operating profit margin is 7.7%, the effect on non-operating items is 0.9, total asset turnover is 1.5, financial leverage is 1.2, and the return on equity is 10%?

    A. 0.6
    B. 0.7
    *C. 0.8 = 10% / [(7.7%)(0.9)(1.5)(1.2)]

78. Which is good corporate governance for voting?

    *A. Votes are counted by a third party
    B. Shareowners must be present to vote
    C. Only management votes for corporate changes

Morning Exam

79. External or informational efficiency means

    A. Low transaction costs
    B. Prices do not change rapidly
    *C. Market prices reflect all available information

80. The minimum pretax income included as a listing requirement for the NYSE in 2004 was $2.5

    *A. Million for the last year and $2.0 million for the last two years
    B. Billion last year and $2.0 billion for the last two years
    C. Trillion last year and $2.0 trillion for the last two years

81. Short sellers

    A. Lend securities
    *B. Borrow securities
    C. Place limit orders

82. For a margin account with an initial deposit of $5,000 used to purchase 200 shares of stock at $50, and a maintenance margin of 25%, what is the margin call closest to if the stock declines to $30?

    A. $0
    *B. $500 = 25%($30)(200) - [$30(200) - $5,000]
    C. $1,000

83. What is closest to the return on the value weighted index for three stocks with prices at the beginning of the year for stocks A, B, and C of $11, $20, and $17, respectively, prices at the end of the year for stocks A, B, and C of $14, $25, and $15, respectively, and 3 million shares of stock A, 20 million shares of stock B, and 6 million shares of stock C?

    A. 12.0%
    B. 13.5%
    *C. 18.1% = [3($14) + 20($25) + 6($15)] / [3($11) + 20($20) + 6($17)] - 1

84. Which form of the efficient market hypothesis (EMH) is tested by time-series analysis, cross-sectional analysis, or event studies?

    A. Weak form
    B. Strong form
    *C. Semi-strong form

Morning Exam

85. Which is least likely to be considered a problem that may prevent arbitrageurs from correcting anomalies?

   A. It is unclear when mispricing will disappear
   *B. Arbitrageurs have an unlimited amount of capital
   C. It is rare to find two assets with exactly the same risk

86. Which is least likely to explain why valid anomalies may not be profitable?

   *A. Conditions governing anomalies are constant
   B. Documented anomalies are based on averages
   C. Positive abnormal returns do not mean positive returns

87. Which is closest to the P/E ratio of a common stock with a dividend payout ratio of 50%, a dividend growth rate of 7%, and a required rate of return of 11%?

   *A. 12.50 = 50% / (11% - 7%)
   B. 13.38
   C. 13.88

88. Which is closest to price of a share using the dividend discount model (DDM) with a dividend payout ratio of 60%, a dividend growth rate of 5.1%, a required rate of return of 12.6%, a weighted-average cost of capital of 12%, and current earnings per share of $2?

   A. $16.00
   *B. $16.82 = [$2 (60%)(1.051) / (12.6% - 5.1%)]
   C. $18.28

89. What is the estimated price of a stock using the dividend discount model if the earnings retention ratio is 50%, the ROE is 20%, the current dividends are $2 per share, and the required rate of return is 15%?

   *A. $44 = $2 (1.1) / (15% - 10%) where 10% = 20% (50%)
   B. $45
   C. $50

90. Which is least likely to be considered a rationale for using price to sales value (P / S) ratios?

   *A. Reflects a company's expenses
   B. Sales are positive even when EPS is negative
   C. Less subject to manipulation than EPS or book value

Morning Exam

91. Which is least likely to be a forward commitment for all parties involved?

    A. Swap
    *B. Put option
    C. Futures contract

92. What is a commitment for one party, the long, to buy a currency at a fixed price from the other party, the short?

    A. Eurodollar time deposit
    *B. Currency forward contract
    C. Forward rate agreement (FRA)

93. What is the ending balance at the end of day 4 for a holder of a short position of 20 futures contracts if the initial futures price on day 0 is $212, the initial margin requirement is $10, the maintenance margin requirement is $7.50, the settlement price on day 1 is $211, the settlement price on day 2 is $214, the settlement price on day 3 is $209, and the settlement price on day 4 is $210?

    A. $160
    B. $220
    *C. $240 = $200 + $20 - $60 + $100 - $20; where $200 is the initial deposit, $20 is the gain on day 1, $60 is the loss on day 2, $100 is the gain on day 3, $20 is the loss on day 4; the ending balances days 0 through 4 are $200, $220, $160, $260, and $240

94. An investor buys a call at $95 for $2 when the price of the stock was $95. What is the intrinsic value of the call if the new price of the stock is $94?

    A. -$1.00
    *B. $0.00; $94 < $95
    C. $1.00

95. An asset manager enters into a $25 million equity swap and agrees to pay a dealer a fixed rate of 4.5% and the dealer agrees to pay the return on a large-cap index. Payments are made semi-annually based on 180 days out of a 365-day year. The value of the large-cap index starts at 578.50. In six months, the small cap index is at 581.35. Which party pays what amount after the payments are netted?

    A. The dealer pays the asset manager $677,958
    *B. The asset manager pays the dealer $431,632 = $25,000,000(4.5%) (180/365) - $25,000,000(581.35/578.50 - 1)
    C. The asset manager pays the dealer $677,958

Morning Exam

96. What is the maximum loss for a covered call option at expiration, for a stock selling for $98 and a call option at $105 selling for $8?

   *A. $90 = $98 - $8
   B. $98
   C. Unlimited

97. What sets forth a formula for calculating the amount the issue must pay to call an issue to protect the yield of investors?

   A. Deferred call
   B. Call schedule
   *C. Make-whole premium

98. What is the price of a bond when the coupon rate is equal to the yield required by the market?

   *A. Equal to par value
   B. Less than par value
   C. Greater then par value

99. What is a security's price sensitivity to changes in yield?

   *A. Duration
   B. Convexity
   C. Dollar duration

100. Which feature is least likely to increase reinvestment risk?

   A. Callable
   B. Amortizing
   *C. Zero-coupon

101. A decrease in expected yield volatility will cause the value of

   A. Callable bonds to decrease
   B. Putable bonds to increase
   *C. Putable bonds to decrease

Morning Exam

102. An investor purchases $10,000 of par value of a Treasury inflation protection security (TIPS). The real rate determined at the auction is 3.8%. If at the end of the first six months the CPI-U is 2.4% on an annual rate and at the end of the second six months the CPI-U is 2.8% on an annual basis, which is closest to the coupon payment at the end of the second six months?

    A. $192.28
    *B. $194.97 = {$10,000 + [$10,000 (2.4%) / 2]} (1 + 2.8%/2) (3.8%/2)
    C. $261.68

103. What are the most common internal credit enhancements for asset-backed securities?

    A. Reserve funds, letter of credit, and bond insurance
    B. Corporate guarantee, letter of credit, and bond insurance
    *C. Reserve funds, over collateralization, and senior/subordinate structures

104. What is the relative yield spread between a 5-year bond with a 5.11% yield and a 5-year on-the-run Treasury with a 4.18% yield?

    A. 93 basis points
    *B. 22.2% = (5.11% - 4.18%) / 4.18%
    C. 1.222

105. As a bond moves closer to maturity, assuming the discount rate does not change, a bond's value

    A. Increases over time if the bond is selling at a premium
    *B. Increases over time if the bond is selling at a discount
    C. Decreases over time if the bond is selling at par

106. At what interest rate do bond cash flows need to be reinvested for an investment to achieve the yield to maturity?

    A. Current yield
    *B. Yield to maturity
    C. Bond-equivalent yield

107. Which is closest to the value of a $100 par, 1.5-year, 6% coupon Treasury bond if the forward rates for the periods 1, 2, and 3 are 3.00%, 3.60%, and 3.92%, respectively?

    A. $96
    B. $102
    *C. $104 = [$3 / 1.015] + [$3 / (1.015)(1.018)] + [$103 / (1.015)(1.018)(1.0196)]

Morning Exam

108. What is a measure of the approximate percentage change in price for a 100 basis point change in rates?

   *A. Duration
   B. Convexity
   C. Price value of a basis point (PVBP)

109. Which is closest to the duration of a portfolio with $200,000 in a bond with a duration of 4; $300,000 in a bond with a duration of 6; $250,000 in a bond with a duration of 7; and $550,000 in a bond with a duration of 8?

   *A. 6.73 = ($200,000 / $1,300,000) 4 + ($300,000 / $1,300,000) 6 + ($250,000 / $1,300,000) 7 + ($550,000 / $1,300,000) 8
   B. 7.06
   C. 7.73

110. Which is closest to percentage price change for a 5% 25-year bond with duration of 14.19 and convexity of 141.68 if yields decrease by 200 basis points?

   A. 22.71%
   B. 28.38%
   *C. 34.05% = 14.19 (.02) + 141.68 (.02)^2

111. What is fee simple real estate?

   A. Mortgaged
   B. Leveraged equity
   *C. Free and clear equity

112. A real estate investment project had a purchase price of $700,000 which is financed 20% by equity and is sold at the end of five years. Which is closest to the internal rate of return (IRR) of the project if the property has after-tax cash flow for the first five years of $21,575, $24,361, $27,280, $30,339, and $273,629, and the present value of after tax cash flows is $164,012 at 22%, $144,303 at 26%, and $127,747 at 30%?

   *A. 27%, based on $0 approximately = $21,575/1.27 + $24,361/1.27^2 + $27,280/1.27^3 + $30,339/1.27^4 + $273,629/1.27^5 - 20%($700,000); IRR = 26.9754%
   B. 28%
   C. 29%

Morning Exam

113. Which is closest to the probability of survival through the end of seven years for a project with a failure probability in year 1 of 0.25, in year 2 of 0.22, and in each of years 3 through 7 of 0.20?

   A. 0.0%
   *B. 19.2% = (1 - 25%)(1 - 22%)(1 - 20%)^5
   C. 80.8%

114. Which statement is least accurate regarding hedge funds?

   A. A hedge fund searches for absolute returns
   B. A hedge fund is an actively managed investment vehicle using a variety of strategies
   *C. All hedge funds offer plays against the market by using short selling, futures, and derivatives

115. Which is the first step in the portfolio management process, before the investment strategy?

   *A. Policy statement
   B. Continual monitoring
   C. Construct the portfolio

116. From 1934 through 2003, during what percentage of one-year holding periods did stock returns trail T-bill returns?

   A. 11.5%
   *B. 35.7%
   C. 64.3%

117. If an investor has a portfolio with equal weights of four securities with returns of 10%, 12%, 16%, and 22%, what will happen to the expected return for the portfolio if the security with the 16% return is replaced with a security with a return equal to the original portfolio?

   A. Increases
   *B. Decreases; (10% + 12% + 16% + 22%) / 4 = 15% > (10% + 12% + 15% + 22%) / 4 = 14.75%
   C. Remains the same

Morning Exam

118. Which is closest to the standard deviation of a portfolio with a 50% weight in each of two securities, both of which have an expected return of 20% and a standard deviation of 10%, if the correlation coefficient is -0.5?

   *A. 5%= [(50%^2)(10%^2) + (50%^2)(10%^2) + 2(50%)(50%)(-0.5)(10%)(10%)]^.5
   B. 7%
   C. 9%

119. Which is least likely to be considered an assumption of capital market theory?

   A. Investors target points on the efficient frontier
   B. Investors can borrow or lend money at the risk-free rate
   *C. Investors estimate different probability distributions for future rates of return

120. Which is closest to the number of securities needed in a portfolio to approach 90% of the variance with complete diversification?

   *A. 15 to 18
   B. 60 to 72
   C. 120 to 144

Afternoon Exam

1. Which topic of the CFA Institute's Standards of Professional Conduct includes knowledge of the law, independence and objectivity, misrepresentation, and misconduct?

   A. Professionalism
   B. Duties to clients
   C. Integrity of capital markets

2. CFA charterholder Sheth is the investment manager of the Rego County Employees Pension Plan. The plan requested proposals for a foreign equity manager, and after the board interviewed the most qualified firms, Sheth went against the staff recommendation and recommended Raman Advisors. A reporter called and asked if the recommendation was related to Raman Advisors being one of the sponsors of an investment fact-finding trip to Asia that Sheth made earlier in the year. The trip was arranged by the Pension Investment Academy. The Academy obtains support for trips from sponsors such as Raman Advisors, then the Academy pays for the expenses of pension fund managers like Sheth. Sheth is least likely to have violated which Standard of Professional Conduct?

   A. Loyalty, prudence, and care
   B. Independence and objectivity
   C. Material nonpublic information

3. CFA charterholder Patel works for a small firm offering investment advice. She assures a potential client who just inherited a large sum of money that her firm can provide all the financial and investment services they need. The firm is qualified to provide investment advice but does not actually offer a full array of financial and investment services. Did Patel violate any Standards of Professional Conduct?

   A. No
   B. Yes, relating to misrepresentation
   C. Yes, relating to independence and objectivity

4. CFA charterholder Kolli volunteers at a charity and makes purchases with the charity's money. Kolli makes an arrangement with a vendor to prepare inflated invoices and split the surcharge. Did Kolli violate any Standards of Professional Conduct?

   A. No
   B. Yes, relating to misconduct
   C. Yes, relating to misrepresentation

Afternoon Exam

5. Which statement is most accurate related to the Standard of Professional Conduct on duties to clients?

    A. Members and candidates must perform services with skill and care
    B. Members and candidates must determine applicable fiduciary duty and must comply with such duty to persons and interests to whom it is owed
    C. Members and candidates who possess material nonpublic information that could affect the value of an investment must not act or cause others to act on the information

6. CFA charterholder Bokil allocates shares from block trades by filling mutual funds orders first then allocating the remaining shares based on portfolio size. Did Bokil violate any Standards of Professional Conduct?

    A. No
    B. Yes, relating to fair dealing
    C. Yes, relating to priority of transactions

7. CFA charterholder Sharmar is the CIO for an insurance company whose investment policy provides for liquid low-risk investments. Sharmar invests a portion of company assets in private equity. Did Sharmar violate any Standards of Professional Conduct?

    A. No
    B. Yes, relating to fair dealing and misrepresentation
    C. Yes, relating to suitability and loyalty, prudence, and care

8. CFA charterholder Kraynak manages money for a business and believes the CFO is embezzling money. What is Kraynak's most appropriate initial response?

    A. Resign as money manager
    B. Disclose the evidence to government officials
    C. Check with his firm's compliance department as well as outside counsel

9. CFA charterholder Chavan leaves a firm to start her own business. She obtains phone numbers of former clients through public records to contact them. Did Chavan violate any Standards of Professional Conduct?

    A. No
    B. Yes, relating to loyalty
    C. Yes, relating to disclosure of conflicts

Afternoon Exam

10. If a member cannot discharge supervisory responsibilities because of the absence of a compliance system or because of an inadequate compliance system, the best action for the member is to

    A. Require that the firm adopt the CFA Code of Ethics
    B. Accept the supervisory responsibility and begin the process of encouraging the firm to adopt reasonable procedures to allow the member to adequately exercise such responsibility
    C. Decline in writing to accept supervisory responsibility until the firm adopts reasonable procedures to allow the member to adequately exercise such responsibility

11. The president of SKA Capital Management changed the firm's investment strategy to emulate the performance of a major market index without informing clients. Did the president violate any Standards of Professional Conduct?

    A. No
    B. Yes, relating to duties to clients
    C. Yes, relating to communications with clients and prospective clients

12. According to the standards, whose accounts have the lowest priority?

    A. Clients
    B. Members
    C. Employers

13. CFA charterholder Laksana attends a closed-circuit broadcast to her firm's branches in which CFA charterholder Khalid makes negative comments about a company. Khalid's comments will be in a report to be published the next day for distribution to clients. Laksana closes out long positions in the stock and buys put options immediately after the broadcast. Did Laksana violate any Standards of Professional Conduct?

    A. No
    B. Yes, related to priority of transactions
    C. Yes, related to communication with clients and prospective clients

Afternoon Exam

14. Five years after receiving the CFA charter, Okah stops paying his CFA Institute dues and does not file a completed Professional Conduct Statement with CFA Institute. He still uses the initials CFA after his name. Did Okah violate any Standards of Professional Conduct?

    A. No
    B. Yes, related to conduct as members and candidates in the CFA program
    C. Yes, related to reference to the CFA Institute, the CFA designation, and the CFA program

15. Which is least likely to ensure fair treatment of clients when a new investment recommendation is made?

    A. Monitor the trading activity of all personnel
    B. Maximize the elapsed time between the decision and the dissemination of a recommendation
    C. Limit the number of people in the firm who are aware in advance that a recommendation is to be disseminated

16. CFA charterholder Rooker recommends the purchase of a mutual fund that invests solely in long-term U.S. Treasury bonds. Rooker tells clients that the payment of the bonds is guaranteed by the U.S. government, and the default risk is virtually zero. Did Rooker violate any Standards of Professional Conduct?

    A. No
    B. Yes, related to misrepresentation
    C. Yes, related to diligence and reasonable basis

17. CFA charterholder Overton is a portfolio manager at Venkatesan Capital who has a beneficial interest in an account he manages for his parents. Overton discloses to his employer his beneficial interest in his parents' account and follows the firm's pre-clearance and reporting requirements. Overton does not undertake transactions in the account until after his clients and employer have had an adequate opportunity to act. Did Overton violate any Standards of Professional Conduct?

    A. No
    B. Yes, related to duties to clients
    C. Yes, related to duties to employers

Afternoon Exam

18. What is the GIPS compliance statement?

    A. [Insert name of firm] has prepared and presented this report in compliance with the Global Investment Performance Standards (GIPS)
    B. [Insert name of firm] has prepared and presented this report in compliance with the Global Investment Performance Standards (GIPS) except for [list exceptional items, if any]
    C. [Insert name of firm] has prepared and presented this report in compliance with the Global Investment Performance Standards (GIPS) published by the CFA Institute and Investment Performance Council

19. What is the lump sum value after 30 years of end-of-year pension contributions of $10,000 if the earnings are 7% per year?

    A. $944,608
    B. $977,669
    C. $1,010,730

20. How should a firm choose when given two independent projects: Project A has an NPV of $4,000 and an IRR of 50%; and Project B has an NPV of $8,000 and an IRR of 40%?

    A. Accept both; they are independent (can invest in both) and both have positive NPVs
    B. Choose Project A
    C. Choose Project B

21. Given 1 observation in the 2% to 4% interval, 3 in the 4% to 6% interval, 4 in the 6% to 8% interval, and 2 in the 8% to 10% interval, what is the relative frequency and cumulative relative frequency of the 4% to 6% interval?

    A. Relative frequency = 30%, cumulative relative frequency = 40%
    B. Relative frequency = 40%, cumulative relative frequency = 30%
    C. Relative frequency = 30%, cumulative relative frequency = 60%

22. What is the first quintile for funds with returns of -20%, -10%, -6%, -5%, 0%, 6%, 12%, 14%, and 20%?

    A. -10%
    B. -8%
    C. -6%

Afternoon Exam

23. What is the positive square root of semivariance?

    A. Target semivariance
    B. Semideviation
    C. Geometric mean

24. What type of distribution has a mean greater than the median which is greater than the mode?

    A. Normal
    B. Positive skew
    C. Negative skew

25. What is a probability based on judgment?

    A. a priori
    B. Empirical
    C. Subjective

26. What is the covariance between stock A and stock B, if there is a 60% probability that stock A will return 5% and stock B will return 10%, and a 40% probability that stock A will return 15% and stock B will return 5%?

    A. -0.24%
    B. -0.12%
    C. 0.24%

27. How many ways can 15 mutual funds be rated so that 2 have five stars, 3 have four stars, 5 have three stars, 3 have two stars, and 2 have one star?

    A. 5,045,040
    B. 12,612,600
    C. 75,675,600

28. If an investment manager has a 50% probability of beating a benchmark each year, what is the probability of beating the benchmark in 0 out of 4 years?

    A. 0.01125
    B. 0.03125
    C. 0.06250

Afternoon Exam

29. If the price for a commodity in three years is predicted to be in the $150 to $200 range, what is the probability the stock will be under $155 in three years, assuming a continuous uniform distribution?

    A. 10%
    B. 20%
    C. 30%

30. Compared to the normal distribution, which is least likely to apply to the lognormal distribution?

    A. Skewed to the left
    B. Skewed to the right
    C. Useful in describing distribution of stock prices

31. Which statistic is appropriate for sampling from a normal distribution with a known variance for a large sample size?

    A. t-statistic
    B. z-statistic
    C. Not available

32. What type of formulation is a "not-equal-to" alternative hypothesis?

    A. Null hypothesis test
    B. One-tailed hypothesis test
    C. Two-tailed hypothesis test

33. What happens to demand for a resource when the price of a substitute resource decreases?

    A. Increases
    B. Decreases
    C. Stays the same

34. Which is the most likely result of a tax when supply is perfectly inelastic?

    A. Price increase and sellers pay the entire tax
    B. Price increase and buyers pay the entire tax
    C. No price increase and sellers pay the entire tax

Afternoon Exam

35. What is the economic profit if total revenue is $400,000, explicit costs are $230,000, forgone wages are $40,000, forgone interest is $20,000, economic depreciation is $25,000, and normal profit is $50,000?

    A. $35,000
    B. $50,000
    C. $85,000

36. What is least likely a reason firms are more efficient than markets as coordinators of economic activity?

    A. Lower transaction costs
    B. Economies of scale
    C. Agents acting in best interest of principals

37. What is least likely to be a characteristic of perfect competition?

    A. Many firms sell identical products to many buyers
    B. There are no restrictions on entry into the industry
    C. Established firms have advantages over new ones

38. Which is least likely to be part of the loss from a monopoly being inefficient?

    A. Sunk costs
    B. Deadweight loss
    C. Rent seeking costs

39. Which occupation is most likely to have an inelastic demand for labor?

    A. Teacher
    B. Assembly line worker
    C. Farm worker

40. What type of unemployment is where workers become obsolete?

    A. Frictional
    B. Structural
    C. Cyclical

41. What is the relationship between real GDP demanded and the price level in the short run?

    A. Inversely correlated
    B. Positively correlated
    C. Independent

Afternoon Exam

42. Which is least likely to be used by the Federal Reserve System to slow the growth of the economy?

    A. Increase the federal funds rate
    B. Buy government securities
    C. Increase reserve requirements

43. Which is least likely to explain the sources of investment finance?

    A. Investment is financed by national saving and borrowing from the rest of the world
    B. Investment is equal to the sum of private saving and government saving
    C. When the government sector has a budget deficit, it contributes toward financing investment

44. Which is least likely to be part of the transmission process after the Federal Reserve System lowers the federal funds rate?

    A. Short term rates and the exchange rate fall
    B. The quantity of money and supply of loanable funds increase
    C. Long term real interest rate rises

45. Where is the statement of retained earnings found?

    A. Balance sheet
    B. Statement of cash flows
    C. Statement of owners' equity

46. Which is a financing activity?

    A. Issuing stock
    B. Cost of providing goods and services
    C. Purchase of property, plant, and equipment

47. Which involves cash movement after accounting recognition?

    A. Prepaid expense
    B. Accrued expense
    C. Unearned revenue

48. What is not a presentation requirement for financial statements under IAS No. 1?

    A. No offsetting
    B. Substance over form
    C. Aggregation where appropriate

Afternoon Exam

49. Under which financial reporting framework is management expressly required to consider the framework if there is no standard or interpretation for the issue?

    A. IFRS but not FASB
    B. FASB but not IFRS
    C. Both IFRS and FASB

50. Which is closest to the profit that will be reported in the first year under the percentage-of-completion method if the revenue is $3 million the first year, $4 million the second year, and $5 million the third year; and the costs are $5 million the first year, $3 million the second year, and $2 million the third year?

    A. $0.5 million
    B. $1.0 million
    C. $1.3 million

51. Which inventory costing method produces the lowest cost of goods sold when prices are rising?

    A. LIFO
    B. FIFO
    C. Weighted average cost

52. Which depreciation method is based on the excess of cost over residual value, divided by the estimated useful life?

    A. Straight-line depreciation
    B. Diminishing balance method
    C. Double declining balance method

53. What would be the outstanding shares at the end of the year for calculating EPS if the board of a company with 1,000,000 shares outstanding on January 1st at the beginning of the year is considering either a 2 for 1 stock split or a 1,000,000 stock dividend on July 1st?

    A. 2,000,000 for the stock split or the stock dividend
    B. 2,000,000 for the stock split or 1,500,000 for the stock dividend
    C. 1,500,000 for the stock split or 2,000,000 for the stock dividend

54. On the balance sheet, what best describes assets expected to be liquidated or used up within one year or one business cycle?

    A. Operating assets
    B. Current assets
    C. Noncurrent assets

Afternoon Exam

55. If cash is $500; marketable securities are $200; receivables are $300; other current assets are $500; and current liabilities are $500, which is closest to the current ratio?

    A. 1
    B. 2
    C. 3

56. Where would conversion of a $1,000 face value bond for $1,000 of common stock most likely be reported on the cash flow statement?

    A. As supplementary information
    B. In the financing category of a cash flow statement
    C. In the financing and investing categories of a cash flow statement

57. Which is closest to cash flows from operations in 2009 if for 2008, retained earnings were $100,000; accounts receivable were $35,000; inventory was $40,000; and accounts payable were $30,000; for 2009, retained earnings were $125,000; accounts receivable were $38,000; inventory was $45,000; and accounts payable were $23,000; and in 2009, the company declared and paid $10,000 in cash dividends and recorded $25,000 in depreciation expense?

    A. $25,000
    B. $35,000
    C. $45,000

58. In a period of declining prices, which is most likely greater for a company that uses FIFO compared to a company that uses LIFO?

    A. Liquidity
    B. Efficiency
    C. Profitability

59. What would most likely be reported for the current period for a company that just acquired research and development costs for a product compared to a company that researched and developed a similar product internally?

    A. Lower assets
    B. Lower net income
    C. Higher cash flow from operations

60. A shorter useful life and lower salvage value

    A. Increase the initial amount of annual depreciation
    B. Decrease the initial amount of annual depreciation
    C. Have no impact on the initial amount of annual depreciation

Afternoon Exam

61. Which is most likely to increase in the year of revaluation for an asset revaluation that increases the value?

    A. Total assets and shareholder's equity, but not depreciation expense
    B. Depreciation expense, but not total assets and shareholder's equity
    C. Total assets, shareholder's equity, and depreciation expense

62. If a U.S. company had current federal income taxes of $28,000, current foreign income taxes of $20,000, deferred federal income taxes of negative $5,000, and deferred foreign income taxes of $1,000, which is closest to the provision for income tax on the U.S. GAAP income statement?

    A. $28,000
    B. $44,000
    C. $48,000

63. Under which are convertible bonds reported at issuance with no separate value attributed to the conversion feature?

    A. U.S. GAAP but not IFRS
    B. IFRS but not U.S. GAAP
    C. Both U.S. GAAP and IFRS

64. Which would most likely explain a decrease in inventory turnover?

    A. More efficient inventory management system
    B. Large write-offs of inventory at the beginning of the period
    C. Operational difficulties resulting in duplicate orders with suppliers

65. What ratios measure the efficiency of a company's operations?

    A. Debt ratios and coverage ratios
    B. Current ratio, quick ratio, cash ratio, and defensive interval ratio
    C. Inventory turnover, days of inventory on hand, receivables turnover, days of sales outstanding, payables turnover, number of days of payables, working capital turnover, fixed asset turnover, and total asset turnover

66. What type of risk factor is related to threats to financial stability and expectations of management?

    A. Opportunities
    B. Incentives/pressures
    C. Attitudes/rationalizations

Afternoon Exam

67. If a U.S. company using LIFO reports inventory of $500,000 and a LIFO reserve of $100,000, what is the inventory closest to after converting to FIFO?

    A. $400,000
    B. $450,000
    C. $600,000

68. Which uses a voting model rather than a dual model based on voting control and economic control to determine need for consolidation when accounting for investments?

    A. IFRS but not U.S. GAAP
    B. U.S. GAAP but not IFRS
    C. Both IFRS and U.S. GAAP

69. What is the net present value for capital budgeting?

    A. The present value of pre-tax cash flows discounted using the cost of debt with investment outlays included as negative cash flows
    B. The present value of after-tax cash flows discounted using the required rate of return with investment outlays included as negative cash flows
    C. The present value of after-tax cash flows discounted using the required rate of return with investment outlays included as positive cash flows

70. What are the NPV and IRR if the initial investment is $25 million, the cash flows are $10 million per year at the end of the each of 3 years, and the required rate of return is 8%?

    A. NPV = negative $0.8 million; IRR = 9.7%
    B. NPV = $0.8 million; IRR = 9.7%
    C. NPV = $0.8 million; IRR = 20.3%

71. Which capital budgeting problem can arise for projects with cash flows that change signs more than once during the project's life?

    A. The multiple IRR problem but not the no IRR problem
    B. The no IRR problem but not the multiple IRR problem
    C. Both the multiple IRR problem and the no IRR problem

Afternoon Exam

72. Which is closest to the after-tax cost of debt using the debt-rating approach if a company sells a 10-year 5% semi-annual coupon AAA rated bond, the marginal tax rate is 40%, and the yield on debt with the same rating is 4%?

    A. 2.4%
    B. 2.6%
    C. 3.0%

73. What is estimated using the CAPM or the dividend discount method?

    A. Cost of equity
    B. Yield to maturity
    C. Cost of preferred stock

74. Which is least likely to be used to estimate the growth rate for the dividend discount model?

    A. Risk-free rate
    B. Published forecasts
    C. Estimate of the sustainable growth rate

75. Which is closest to the country risk premium if the bond yield for a 10-year government bond in the country is 10.5% compared to 4.5% for a similar U.S. Treasury bond, the annualized standard deviation of the equity index in the country is 35%, and the standard deviation of the country's bond market in terms of the U.S. dollar is 25%?

    A. 4.3%
    B. 6.0%
    C. 8.4%

76. Which is least likely to indicate greater liquidity?

    A. Lower number of days of payables
    B. Lower number of days of receivables
    C. Lower number of days of inventory

77. Which is closest to return on equity using DuPont analysis if, in millions, operating income is $530, revenues are $13,565, income before taxes is $461, taxes are $126, average total assets are $6,767, and average shareholders' equity is $3,223?

    A. 10.39%
    B. 14.30%
    C. 14.64%

Afternoon Exam

78. Which is least likely to be sales driven on a pro forma income statement?

    A. Cost of sales
    B. Interest expense
    C. Operating expenses

79. Which means that prices do not change much from one transaction to the next?

    A. Liquidity
    B. Marketability
    C. Price continuity

80. Who uses their exchange membership to buy and sell for their own accounts?

    A. Floor brokers
    B. Registered traders
    C. Commission brokers

81. At what price is a market order to buy executed?

    A. Lowest ask price
    B. Lowest bid price
    C. Highest bid price

82. For a margin account with an initial deposit of $5,000, a purchase of 300 shares at $30, and a maintenance margin of 30%, what is the price at which the investor will get a margin call?

    A. $19.05
    B. $23.08
    C. $23.81

83. Which bond indexes include bonds with correlations averaging about 0.95?

    A. EAFE
    B. Global government bond indexes
    C. U.S. investment-grade bond indexes

84. Which is least likely to be considered an anomaly with respect to the semi-strong from of the EMH?

    A. Abnormal returns from high P/E stocks
    B. Abnormal returns following earnings surprises
    C. Abnormal returns in January compared to December

Afternoon Exam

85. Removing what types of firms makes the January effect disappear?

    A. Small firms
    B. Large firms
    C. Firms no longer in existence

86. Which is closest to the value of common stock with next year's dividend expected to be $1, a dividend growth rate of 7%, and a required rate of return of 12%?

    A. $20.00
    B. $21.40
    C. $22.40

87. Which is least likely to result in a higher value of common stock using the earnings multiplier model?

    A. Higher dividend payout ratio
    B. Lower required rate of return
    C. Lower growth rate of dividends

88. What is the growth rate of equity earnings without any external financing?

    A. Payout ratio times the rate of return on equity capital
    B. Retention rate times the rate of return on equity capital
    C. Payout ratio times the weighted average cost of capital

89. Which is least likely to be considered a drawback of using price to earnings (P/E) ratios?

    A. EPS can be negative
    B. Earnings often have volatile, transient components
    C. Differences in P/Es may be related to differences in long-run average returns

90. A company had EPS of $1.16 for 2004, $0.62 for 2005, $1.28 for 2006, $1.60 for 2007, and -$1.30 for 2008; book value per share (BVPS) of $8.48 for 2004, $8.92 for 2005, $16.40 for 2006, $19.28 for 2007, and $16.30 for 2008; and ROE of 14% for 2004, 7% for 2005, 8% for 2006, and 8% for 2007. If the current market price is $40, what is the normalized P/E based on the method of average ROE?

    A. 26.5
    B. 32.8
    C. 34.2

Afternoon Exam

91. A derivative is most accurately described as a financial instrument that provides

    A. A return based on an underlying asset
    B. An adjustment to another asset's level of risk
    C. An agreement between two parties to provide something to the other

92. Which is least likely to be a forward commitment for all parties involved?

    A. Swap
    B. Call option
    C. Forward contract

93. What is the ending balance at the end of day 3 for a holder of a short position of 10 futures contracts if the initial futures price on day 0 is $100, the initial margin requirement is 5%, the maintenance margin requirement is 3%, the settlement price on day 1 is $99.2, the settlement price on day 2 is $96, and the settlement price on day 3 is $101?

    A. $40
    B. $90
    C. $100

94. An investor goes long one futures contract at $50 with 2 days to expiration. The settlement price 1 day before expiration is $52 and the mark to market profit is $2. The settlement price at expiration is $53. How is the futures contract terminated by closeout?

    A. Receive $53 - $52 = $1
    B. Pay $52, receive asset worth $53
    C. Sell contract at $53 for a mark to market profit of $53 - $52 = $1

95. What has a specified rate for the exercise rate and a variable rate for the underlying rate?

    A. Put option
    B. Call option
    C. Interest rate option

Afternoon Exam

96. An asset manager enters into a $100 million equity swap and agrees to pay a dealer the return on a stock index and the dealer agrees to pay a fixed rate of 4%. Payments are made semi-annually based on 180 days out of a 365-day year. The value of the stock index starts at 280. In six months, the stock index is at 250. Which party pays what amount after the payments are netted?

   A. The dealer pays the asset manager about $13 million
   B. The dealer pays the asset manager about $9 million
   C. The asset manager pays the dealer about $9 million

97. What does an indenture set forth?

   A. The rights of the issuer and the bondholders
   B. The rights of the issuer and the promises of the bondholders
   C. The promises of the issuer and the rights of the bondholders

98. Which imbedded option is least likely to be considered an advantage to the issuer?

   A. Call provision
   B. Cap on a floater
   C. Conversion privilege

99. Which bond most likely has the least interest rate risk?

   A. Floating rate bond
   B. Zero-coupon bond
   C. 2% fixed coupon bond

100. Which is closest to the duration of a bond if the current price is 90, the price if yields decline by 25 basis points is 92.7, and the price if yields rise by 25 basis points is 88?

   A. 5.20
   B. 10.40
   C. 10.44

101. Which is least likely to be considered credit risk?

   A. Default risk
   B. Inflation risk
   C. Downgrade risk

Afternoon Exam

102. What are created by stripping the coupons and principal payments from Treasury securities?

    A. TIPS
    B. Notes
    C. Zero-coupon Treasury instruments

103. What are bonds escrowed or collateralized by Treasury securities?

    A. Insured bonds
    B. Revenue bonds
    C. Prefunded bonds

104. Which tools of the Federal Reserve are used most often?

    A. Engaging in open market operations and changing the discount rate
    B. Engaging in open market operations and changing the bank reserve requirements
    C. Changing the bank reserve requirements and verbal persuasion to influence how bankers supply credit

105. If the ratio of the yield between two bonds is 1.1 and the yield on the higher quality bond is 5%, which is closest to the yield on the lower quality bond?

    A. 4.5%
    B. 5.5%
    C. 6.5%

106. Which is closest to the value of a 5-year 7% coupon bond with a maturity value of $100 discounted for a 5% annual discount rate on a semiannual basis?

    A. $108.75
    B. $112.10
    C. $115.44

107. If the spot rates on an annual basis are 3.0% for 6 months, 3.3% for 1 year, and 3.5% for 1.5 years, which is closest to the price of a $100 par, 3.5% coupon 1.5-year Treasury security?

    A. $98
    B. $99
    C. $100

Afternoon Exam

108. For an 8% option-free bond, the price changes by 3% if the rates rise 50 basis points. What is the change if rates fall by 50 basis points?

    A. Less than 3%
    B. Exactly 3%
    C. More than 3%

109. How good is an estimated new price using duration likely to be for a 10 basis point increase in yield?

    A. Estimated price close to new price
    B. Overestimates new price by over 10%
    C. Underestimates new price by over 10%

110. Which is closest to percentage price change for a bond with modified duration of 6.5 and convexity of -42.4 if yields increase by 200 basis points?

    A. -14.70%
    B. -13.42%
    C. -6.92%

111. Which is least likely to be considered a disadvantage of exchange-traded funds (ETFs)?

    A. Transparency
    B. Cost-effectiveness
    C. Narrow bid-ask spreads

112. Which is least accurate regarding real estate investments?

    A. Illiquid
    B. Low transaction costs and high market efficiencies
    C. Not directly comparable to other properties, only approximately comparable

113. Which is most accurate regarding real estate appraisals?

    A. Real estate appraisals show frequent changes
    B. An appraisal-based index understates volatility
    C. A spuriously low volatility decreases the attractiveness of real estate

114. Which characteristic is least accurate in describing distressed-securities investing?

    A. The possibility of alpha from mispricing
    B. Liquid with short-term commitment period
    C. Requires intense investor participation and consulting

Afternoon Exam

115. Which investment strategy is most appropriate for building retirement or college education funds?

    A. Current income
    B. Capital preservation
    C. Capital appreciation

116. Which countries had the highest equity allocations in pension fund portfolios in 1998?

    A. Japan and Germany
    B. Ireland and the United States
    C. Hong Kong and the United Kingdom

117. What is the correlation coefficient if the covariance is 0.06%, and the standard deviations of the two individual return indexes are 2% and 3%?

    A. -1
    B. 0
    C. 1

118. Which is closest to the standard deviation of a portfolio with a 60% weight in a security with an expected return of 10% and a standard deviation of 3%, and a 40% weight in a security with an expected return of 15% and a standard deviation of 5%, if the correlation coefficient is 1.00?

    A. 3.0%
    B. 3.6%
    C. 3.8%

119. Which statement about portfolio risk and diversification is least accurate?

    A. Systematic risk cannot be eliminated through diversification
    B. Unsystematic risk can be significantly reduced through diversification
    C. Diversification results from combining securities with perfect correlations

120. If the risk free rate is 5%, the return on the market portfolio is 9%, beta is -0.30, the current stock price is $50, and the expected price in one year is $53, the stock is

    A. Overvalued
    B. Undervalued
    C. Properly valued

Afternoon Exam

1. A	41. A	81. A
2. C	42. B	82. A
3. B	43. C	83. C
4. B	44. C	84. A
5. B	45. C	85. A
6. B	46. A	86. A
7. C	47. B	87. C
8. C	48. B	88. B
9. A	49. A	89. C
10. C	50. B	90. A
11. C	51. B	91. A
12. B	52. A	92. B
13. B	53. A	93. A
14. C	54. B	94. C
15. B	55. C	95. C
16. A	56. A	96. A
17. A	57. C	97. C
18. A	58. B	98. C
19. A	59. B	99. A
20. A	60. A	100. C
21. A	61. C	101. B
22. A	62. B	102. C
23. B	63. A	103. C
24. B	64. C	104. A
25. C	65. C	105. B
26. B	66. B	106. A
27. C	67. C	107. C
28. C	68. A	108. C
29. A	69. B	109. A
30. A	70. B	110. A
31. B	71. C	111. C
32. C	72. A	112. B
33. B	73. A	113. B
34. C	74. A	114. B
35. A	75. C	115. C
36. C	76. A	116. C
37. C	77. A	117. C
38. A	78. B	118. C
39. A	79. C	119. C
40. B	80. B	120. B

Afternoon Exam

1. Which topic of the CFA Institute's Standards of Professional Conduct includes knowledge of the law, independence and objectivity, misrepresentation, and misconduct?

    *A. Professionalism
    B. Duties to clients
    C. Integrity of capital markets

2. CFA charterholder Sheth is the investment manager of the Rego County Employees Pension Plan. The plan requested proposals for a foreign equity manager, and after the board interviewed the most qualified firms, Sheth went against the staff recommendation and recommended Raman Advisors. A reporter called and asked if the recommendation was related to Raman Advisors being one of the sponsors of an investment fact-finding trip to Asia that Sheth made earlier in the year. The trip was arranged by the Pension Investment Academy. The Academy obtains support for trips from sponsors such as Raman Advisors, then the Academy pays for the expenses of pension fund managers like Sheth. Sheth is least likely to have violated which Standard of Professional Conduct?

    A. Loyalty, prudence, and care
    B. Independence and objectivity
    *C. Material nonpublic information (Standard I(B) - independence and objectivity)

3. CFA charterholder Patel works for a small firm offering investment advice. She assures a potential client who just inherited a large sum of money that her firm can provide all the financial and investment services they need. The firm is qualified to provide investment advice but does not actually offer a full array of financial and investment services. Did Patel violate any Standards of Professional Conduct?

    A. No
    *B. Yes, relating to misrepresentation (Standard I(C) - misrepresentation)
    C. Yes, relating to independence and objectivity

4. CFA charterholder Kolli volunteers at a charity and makes purchases with the charity's money. Kolli makes an arrangement with a vendor to prepare inflated invoices and split the surcharge. Did Kolli violate any Standards of Professional Conduct?

    A. No
    *B. Yes, relating to misconduct (Standard I(D) - misconduct)
    C. Yes, relating to misrepresentation

Afternoon Exam

5. Which statement is most accurate related to the Standard of Professional Conduct on duties to clients?

    A. Members and candidates must perform services with skill and care
    *B. Members and candidates must determine applicable fiduciary duty and must comply with such duty to persons and interests to whom it is owed
    C. Members and candidates who possess material nonpublic information that could affect the value of an investment must not act or cause others to act on the information

6. CFA charterholder Bokil allocates shares from block trades by filling mutual funds orders first then allocating the remaining shares based on portfolio size. Did Bokil violate any Standards of Professional Conduct?

    A. No
    *B. Yes, relating to fair dealing (Standard III(B) - fair dealing)
    C. Yes, relating to priority of transactions

7. CFA charterholder Sharmar is the CIO for an insurance company whose investment policy provides for liquid low-risk investments. Sharmar invests a portion of company assets in private equity. Did Sharmar violate any Standards of Professional Conduct?

    A. No
    B. Yes, relating to fair dealing and misrepresentation
    *C. Yes, relating to suitability and loyalty, prudence, and care (Standard III(C) - suitability and Standard III(A) - loyalty, prudence, and care)

8. CFA charterholder Kraynak manages money for a business and believes the CFO is embezzling money. What is Kraynak's most appropriate initial response?

    A. Resign as money manager
    B. Disclose the evidence to government officials
    *C. Check with his firm's compliance department as well as outside counsel (Standard III(E) - preservation of confidentiality)

9. CFA charterholder Chavan leaves a firm to start her own business. She obtains phone numbers of former clients through public records to contact them. Did Chavan violate any Standards of Professional Conduct?

    *A. No (Standard IV(A) - loyalty)
    B. Yes, relating to loyalty
    C. Yes, relating to disclosure of conflicts

Afternoon Exam

10. If a member cannot discharge supervisory responsibilities because of the absence of a compliance system or because of an inadequate compliance system, the best action for the member is to

    A. Require that the firm adopt the CFA Code of Ethics
    B. Accept the supervisory responsibility and begin the process of encouraging the firm to adopt reasonable procedures to allow the member to adequately exercise such responsibility
    *C. Decline in writing to accept supervisory responsibility until the firm adopts reasonable procedures to allow the member to adequately exercise such responsibility (Standard IV(C) - responsibilities of supervisors)

11. The president of SKA Capital Management changed the firm's investment strategy to emulate the performance of a major market index without informing clients. Did the president violate any Standards of Professional Conduct?

    A. No
    B. Yes, relating to duties to clients
    *C. Yes, relating to communications with clients and prospective clients (Standard V(B) - communications with clients and prospective clients)

12. According to the standards, whose accounts have the lowest priority?

    A. Clients
    *B. Members (Standard VI(B) - priority of transactions)
    C. Employers

13. CFA charterholder Laksana attends a closed-circuit broadcast to her firm's branches in which CFA charterholder Khalid makes negative comments about a company. Khalid's comments will be in a report to be published the next day for distribution to clients. Laksana closes out long positions in the stock and buys put options immediately after the broadcast. Did Laksana violate any Standards of Professional Conduct?

    A. No
    *B. Yes, related to priority of transactions (Standard VI(B) - priority of transactions)
    C. Yes, related to communication with clients and prospective clients

Afternoon Exam

14. Five years after receiving the CFA charter, Okah stops paying his CFA Institute dues and does not file a completed Professional Conduct Statement with CFA Institute. He still uses the initials CFA after his name. Did Okah violate any Standards of Professional Conduct?

    A. No
    B. Yes, related to conduct as members and candidates in the CFA program
    *C. Yes, related to reference to the CFA Institute, the CFA designation, and the CFA program (Standard VII(B) - reference to the CFA Institute, the CFA designation, and the CFA program)

15. Which is least likely to ensure fair treatment of clients when a new investment recommendation is made?

    A. Monitor the trading activity of all personnel
    *B. Maximize the elapsed time between the decision and the dissemination of a recommendation (Standard III(B) - fair dealing)
    C. Limit the number of people in the firm who are aware in advance that a recommendation is to be disseminated

16. CFA charterholder Rooker recommends the purchase of a mutual fund that invests solely in long-term U.S. Treasury bonds. Rooker tells clients that the payment of the bonds is guaranteed by the U.S. government, and the default risk is virtually zero. Did Rooker violate any Standards of Professional Conduct?

    *A. No (Standard I(C) - misrepresentation)
    B. Yes, related to misrepresentation
    C. Yes, related to diligence and reasonable basis

17. CFA charterholder Overton is a portfolio manager at Venkatesan Capital who has a beneficial interest in an account he manages for his parents. Overton discloses to his employer his beneficial interest in his parents' account and follows the firm's pre-clearance and reporting requirements. Overton does not undertake transactions in the account until after his clients and employer have had an adequate opportunity to act. Did Overton violate any Standards of Professional Conduct?

    *A. No (Standard III - duties to clients and Standard IV - duties to employers)
    B. Yes, related to duties to clients
    C. Yes, related to duties to employers

Afternoon Exam

18. What is the GIPS compliance statement?

    *A. [Insert name of firm] has prepared and presented this report in compliance with the Global Investment Performance Standards (GIPS)
    B. [Insert name of firm] has prepared and presented this report in compliance with the Global Investment Performance Standards (GIPS) except for [list exceptional items, if any]
    C. [Insert name of firm] has prepared and presented this report in compliance with the Global Investment Performance Standards (GIPS) published by the CFA Institute and Investment Performance Council

19. What is the lump sum value after 30 years of end-of-year pension contributions of $10,000 if the earnings are 7% per year?

    *A. $944,608 = $10,000 [1.07^30 - 1]/.07; n = 30, i = 7, PMT = 10,000; FV = $944,608
    B. $977,669
    C. $1,010,730

20. How should a firm choose when given two independent projects: Project A has an NPV of $4,000 and an IRR of 50%; and Project B has an NPV of $8,000 and an IRR of 40%?

    *A. Accept both; they are independent (can invest in both) and both have positive NPVs
    B. Choose Project A
    C. Choose Project B

21. Given 1 observation in the 2% to 4% interval, 3 in the 4% to 6% interval, 4 in the 6% to 8% interval, and 2 in the 8% to 10% interval, what is the relative frequency and cumulative relative frequency of the 4% to 6% interval?

    *A. Relative frequency = 30%, cumulative relative frequency = 40%
    B. Relative frequency = 40%, cumulative relative frequency = 30%
    C. Relative frequency = 30%, cumulative relative frequency = 60%

22. What is the first quintile for funds with returns of -20%, -10%, -6%, -5%, 0%, 6%, 12%, 14%, and 20%?

    *A. -10%
    B. -8%
    C. -6%

Afternoon Exam

23. What is the positive square root of semivariance?

    A. Target semivariance
    *B. Semideviation
    C. Geometric mean

24. What type of distribution has a mean greater than the median which is greater than the mode?

    A. Normal
    *B. Positive skew
    C. Negative skew

25. What is a probability based on judgment?

    A. a priori
    B. Empirical
    *C. Subjective

26. What is the covariance between stock A and stock B, if there is a 60% probability that stock A will return 5% and stock B will return 10%, and a 40% probability that stock A will return 15% and stock B will return 5%?

    A. -0.24%
    *B. -0.12% = .6(5%-9%)(10%-8%)+.4(15%-9%)(5%-8%)
    C. 0.24%

27. How many ways can 15 mutual funds be rated so that 2 have five stars, 3 have four stars, 5 have three stars, 3 have two stars, and 2 have one star?

    A. 5,045,040
    B. 12,612,600
    *C. 75,675,600 = 15! / [(2!) (3!) (5!) (3!) (2!)]

28. If an investment manager has a 50% probability of beating a benchmark each year, what is the probability of beating the benchmark in 0 out of 4 years?

    A. 0.01125
    B. 0.03125
    *C. 0.06250 = .5^4

Afternoon Exam

29. If the price for a commodity in three years is predicted to be in the $150 to $200 range, what is the probability the stock will be under $155 in three years, assuming a continuous uniform distribution?

    *A. 10% = 5/50
    B. 20%
    C. 30%

30. Compared to the normal distribution, which is least likely to apply to the lognormal distribution?

    *A. Skewed to the left
    B. Skewed to the right
    C. Useful in describing distribution of stock prices

31. Which statistic is appropriate for sampling from a normal distribution with a known variance for a large sample size?

    A. t-statistic
    *B. z-statistic
    C. Not available

32. What type of formulation is a "not-equal-to" alternative hypothesis?

    A. Null hypothesis test
    B. One-tailed hypothesis test
    *C. Two-tailed hypothesis test

33. What happens to demand for a resource when the price of a substitute resource decreases?

    A. Increases
    *B. Decreases
    C. Stays the same

34. Which is the most likely result of a tax when supply is perfectly inelastic?

    A. Price increase and sellers pay the entire tax
    B. Price increase and buyers pay the entire tax
    *C. No price increase and sellers pay the entire tax

Afternoon Exam

35. What is the economic profit if total revenue is $400,000, explicit costs are $230,000, forgone wages are $40,000, forgone interest is $20,000, economic depreciation is $25,000, and normal profit is $50,000?

    *A. $35,000
    B. $50,000
    C. $85,000

36. What is least likely a reason firms are more efficient than markets as coordinators of economic activity?

    A. Lower transaction costs
    B. Economies of scale
    *C. Agents acting in best interest of principals

37. What is least likely to be a characteristic of perfect competition?

    A. Many firms sell identical products to many buyers
    B. There are no restrictions on entry into the industry
    *C. Established firms have advantages over new ones

38. Which is least likely to be part of the loss from a monopoly being inefficient?

    *A. Sunk costs
    B. Deadweight loss
    C. Rent seeking costs

39. Which occupation is most likely to have an inelastic demand for labor?

    *A. Teacher
    B. Assembly line worker
    C. Farm worker

40. What type of unemployment is where workers become obsolete?

    A. Frictional
    *B. Structural
    C. Cyclical

41. What is the relationship between real GDP demanded and the price level in the short run?

    *A. Inversely correlated
    B. Positively correlated
    C. Independent

Afternoon Exam

42. Which is least likely to be used by the Federal Reserve System to slow the growth of the economy?

    A. Increase the federal funds rate
    *B. Buy government securities
    C. Increase reserve requirements

43. Which is least likely to explain the sources of investment finance?

    A. Investment is financed by national saving and borrowing from the rest of the world
    B. Investment is equal to the sum of private saving and government saving
    *C. When the government sector has a budget deficit, it contributes toward financing investment

44. Which is least likely to be part of the transmission process after the Federal Reserve System lowers the federal funds rate?

    A. Short term rates and the exchange rate fall
    B. The quantity of money and supply of loanable funds increase
    *C. Long term real interest rate rises

45. Where is the statement of retained earnings found?

    A. Balance sheet
    B. Statement of cash flows
    *C. Statement of owners' equity

46. Which is a financing activity?

    *A. Issuing stock
    B. Cost of providing goods and services
    C. Purchase of property, plant, and equipment

47. Which involves cash movement after accounting recognition?

    A. Prepaid expense
    *B. Accrued expense
    C. Unearned revenue

48. What is not a presentation requirement for financial statements under IAS No. 1?

    A. No offsetting
    *B. Substance over form
    C. Aggregation where appropriate

Afternoon Exam

49. Under which financial reporting framework is management expressly required to consider the framework if there is no standard or interpretation for the issue?

    *A. IFRS but not FASB
    B. FASB but not IFRS
    C. Both IFRS and FASB

50. Which is closest to the profit that will be reported in the first year under the percentage-of-completion method if the revenue is $3 million the first year, $4 million the second year, and $5 million the third year; and the costs are $5 million the first year, $3 million the second year, and $2 million the third year?

    A. $0.5 million
    *B. $1.0 million = ($5/$10) $12 million - $5 million
    C. $1.3 million

51. Which inventory costing method produces the lowest cost of goods sold when prices are rising?

    A. LIFO
    *B. FIFO
    C. Weighted average cost

52. Which depreciation method is based on the excess of cost over residual value, divided by the estimated useful life?

    *A. Straight-line depreciation
    B. Diminishing balance method
    C. Double declining balance method

53. What would be the outstanding shares at the end of the year for calculating EPS if the board of a company with 1,000,000 shares outstanding on January 1st at the beginning of the year is considering either a 2 for 1 stock split or a 1,000,000 stock dividend on July 1st?

    *A. 2,000,000 for the stock split or the stock dividend
    B. 2,000,000 for the stock split or 1,500,000 for the stock dividend
    C. 1,500,000 for the stock split or 2,000,000 for the stock dividend

54. On the balance sheet, what best describes assets expected to be liquidated or used up within one year or one business cycle?

    A. Operating assets
    *B. Current assets
    C. Noncurrent assets

Afternoon Exam

55. If cash is $500; marketable securities are $200; receivables are $300; other current assets are $500; and current liabilities are $500, which is closest to the current ratio?

   A. 1
   B. 2
   *C. 3 = ($500 + $200 + $300 + $500) / $500

56. Where would conversion of a $1,000 face value bond for $1,000 of common stock most likely be reported on the cash flow statement?

   *A. As supplementary information
   B. In the financing category of a cash flow statement
   C. In the financing and investing categories of a cash flow statement

57. Which is closest to cash flows from operations in 2009 if for 2008, retained earnings were $100,000; accounts receivable were $35,000; inventory was $40,000; and accounts payable were $30,000; for 2009, retained earnings were $125,000; accounts receivable were $38,000; inventory was $45,000; and accounts payable were $23,000; and in 2009, the company declared and paid $10,000 in cash dividends and recorded $25,000 in depreciation expense?

   A. $25,000
   B. $35,000
   *C. $45,000 = $125,000 - $100,000 + $10,000 + $25,000 - ($38,000 - $35,000) - ($45,000 - $40,000) + ($23,000 - $30,000)

58. In a period of declining prices, which is most likely greater for a company that uses FIFO compared to a company that uses LIFO?

   A. Liquidity
   *B. Efficiency
   C. Profitability

59. What would most likely be reported for the current period for a company that just acquired research and development costs for a product compared to a company that researched and developed a similar product internally?

   A. Lower assets
   *B. Lower net income
   C. Higher cash flow from operations

Afternoon Exam

60. A shorter useful life and lower salvage value

    *A. Increase the initial amount of annual depreciation
    B. Decrease the initial amount of annual depreciation
    C. Have no impact on the initial amount of annual depreciation

61. Which is most likely to increase in the year of revaluation for an asset revaluation that increases the value?

    A. Total assets and shareholder's equity, but not depreciation expense
    B. Depreciation expense, but not total assets and shareholder's equity
    *C. Total assets, shareholder's equity, and depreciation expense

62. If a U.S. company had current federal income taxes of $28,000, current foreign income taxes of $20,000, deferred federal income taxes of negative $5,000, and deferred foreign income taxes of $1,000, which is closest to the provision for income tax on the U.S. GAAP income statement?

    A. $28,000
    *B. $44,000 = $28,000 + $20,000 - $5,000 + $1,000
    C. $48,000

63. Under which are convertible bonds reported at issuance with no separate value attributed to the conversion feature?

    *A. U.S. GAAP but not IFRS
    B. IFRS but not U.S. GAAP
    C. Both U.S. GAAP and IFRS

64. Which would most likely explain a decrease in inventory turnover?

    A. More efficient inventory management system
    B. Large write-offs of inventory at the beginning of the period
    *C. Operational difficulties resulting in duplicate orders with suppliers

65. What ratios measure the efficiency of a company's operations?

    A. Debt ratios and coverage ratios
    B. Current ratio, quick ratio, cash ratio, and defensive interval ratio
    *C. Inventory turnover, days of inventory on hand, receivables turnover, days of sales outstanding, payables turnover, number of days of payables, working capital turnover, fixed asset turnover, and total asset turnover

Afternoon Exam

66. What type of risk factor is related to threats to financial stability and expectations of management?

    A. Opportunities
    *B. Incentives/pressures
    C. Attitudes/rationalizations

67. If a U.S. company using LIFO reports inventory of $500,000 and a LIFO reserve of $100,000, what is the inventory closest to after converting to FIFO?

    A. $400,000
    B. $450,000
    *C. $600,000

68. Which uses a voting model rather than a dual model based on voting control and economic control to determine need for consolidation when accounting for investments?

    *A. IFRS but not U.S. GAAP
    B. U.S. GAAP but not IFRS
    C. Both IFRS and U.S. GAAP

69. What is the net present value for capital budgeting?

    A. The present value of pre-tax cash flows discounted using the cost of debt with investment outlays included as negative cash flows
    *B. The present value of after-tax cash flows discounted using the required rate of return with investment outlays included as negative cash flows
    C. The present value of after-tax cash flows discounted using the required rate of return with investment outlays included as positive cash flows

70. What are the NPV and IRR if the initial investment is $25 million, the cash flows are $10 million per year at the end of the each of 3 years, and the required rate of return is 8%?

    A. NPV = negative $0.8 million; IRR = 9.7%
    *B. NPV = $0.8 million; IRR = 9.7%, NPV = $10 / 1.08 + $10 / 1.08^2 + $10 / 1.08^3 - $25; IRR = 9.7% where $10 / 1.097 + $10 / 1.097^2 + $10 / 1.097^3 = $25; NPV: n =3, i = 8, PMT = 10, FV = 0; PV = 25.8, NPV = $25.8 - $25 = $0.8; IRR: n =3, PV = -25, PMT = 10, FV = 0; i = 9.7, IRR = 9.7%
    C. NPV = $0.8 million; IRR = 20.3%

Afternoon Exam

71. Which capital budgeting problem can arise for projects with cash flows that change signs more than once during the project's life?

    A. The multiple IRR problem but not the no IRR problem
    B. The no IRR problem but not the multiple IRR problem
    *C. Both the multiple IRR problem and the no IRR problem

72. Which is closest to the after-tax cost of debt using the debt-rating approach if a company sells a 10-year 5% semi-annual coupon AAA rated bond, the marginal tax rate is 40%, and the yield on debt with the same rating is 4%?

    *A. 2.4% = 4% (1-40%)
    B. 2.6%
    C. 3.0%

73. What is estimated using the CAPM or the dividend discount method?

    *A. Cost of equity
    B. Yield to maturity
    C. Cost of preferred stock

74. Which is least likely to be used to estimate the growth rate for the dividend discount model?

    *A. Risk-free rate
    B. Published forecasts
    C. Estimate of the sustainable growth rate

75. Which is closest to the country risk premium if the bond yield for a 10-year government bond in the country is 10.5% compared to 4.5% for a similar U.S. Treasury bond, the annualized standard deviation of the equity index in the country is 35%, and the standard deviation of the country's bond market in terms of the U.S. dollar is 25%?

    A. 4.3%
    B. 6.0%
    *C. 8.4% = (10.5% - 4.5%)(35%/25%)

76. Which is least likely to indicate greater liquidity?

    *A. Lower number of days of payables
    B. Lower number of days of receivables
    C. Lower number of days of inventory

Afternoon Exam

77. Which is closest to return on equity using DuPont analysis if, in millions, operating income is $530, revenues are $13,565, income before taxes is $461, taxes are $126, average total assets are $6,767, and average shareholders' equity is $3,223?

   *A. 10.39% = ($461 - $126) / $3,223
   B. 14.30%
   C. 14.64%

78. Which is least likely to be sales driven on a pro forma income statement?

   A. Cost of sales
   *B. Interest expense
   C. Operating expenses

79. Which means that prices do not change much from one transaction to the next?

   A. Liquidity
   B. Marketability
   *C. Price continuity

80. Who uses their exchange membership to buy and sell for their own accounts?

   A. Floor brokers
   *B. Registered traders
   C. Commission brokers

81. At what price is a market order to buy executed?

   *A. Lowest ask price
   B. Lowest bid price
   C. Highest bid price

82. For a margin account with an initial deposit of $5,000, a purchase of 300 shares at $30, and a maintenance margin of 30%, what is the price at which the investor will get a margin call?

   *A. $19.05 = $30 (1 - ($5,000/$9,000)) / (1 - 30%); [300($19.05) - $4,000] / [300($19.05)] = 30%
   B. $23.08
   C. $23.81

Afternoon Exam

83. Which bond indexes include bonds with correlations averaging about 0.95?

    A. EAFE
    B. Global government bond indexes
    *C. U.S. investment-grade bond indexes

84. Which is least likely to be considered an anomaly with respect to the semi-strong from of the EMH?

    *A. Abnormal returns from high P/E stocks
    B. Abnormal returns following earnings surprises
    C. Abnormal returns in January compared to December

85. Removing what types of firms makes the January effect disappear?

    *A. Small firms
    B. Large firms
    C. Firms no longer in existence

86. Which is closest to the value of common stock with next year's dividend expected to be $1, a dividend growth rate of 7%, and a required rate of return of 12%?

    *A. $20.00 = $1 / (12% - 7%)
    B. $21.40
    C. $22.40

87. Which is least likely to result in a higher value of common stock using the earnings multiplier model?

    A. Higher dividend payout ratio
    B. Lower required rate of return
    *C. Lower growth rate of dividends

88. What is the growth rate of equity earnings without any external financing?

    A. Payout ratio times the rate of return on equity capital
    *B. Retention rate times the rate of return on equity capital
    C. Payout ratio times the weighted average cost of capital

89. Which is least likely to be considered a drawback of using price to earnings (P/E) ratios?

    A. EPS can be negative
    B. Earnings often have volatile, transient components
    *C. Differences in P/Es may be related to differences in long-run average returns

Afternoon Exam

90. A company had EPS of $1.16 for 2004, $0.62 for 2005, $1.28 for 2006, $1.60 for 2007, and -$1.30 for 2008; book value per share (BVPS) of $8.48 for 2004, $8.92 for 2005, $16.40 for 2006, $19.28 for 2007, and $16.30 for 2008; and ROE of 14% for 2004, 7% for 2005, 8% for 2006, and 8% for 2007. If the current market price is $40, what is the normalized P/E based on the method of average ROE?

   *A. 26.5 = $40 / {[(14% + 7% + 8% + 8%) / 4]($16.3)}
   B. 32.8
   C. 34.2

91. A derivative is most accurately described as a financial instrument that provides

   *A. A return based on an underlying asset
   B. An adjustment to another asset's level of risk
   C. An agreement between two parties to provide something to the other

92. Which is least likely to be a forward commitment for all parties involved?

   A. Swap
   *B. Call option
   C. Forward contract

93. What is the ending balance at the end of day 3 for a holder of a short position of 10 futures contracts if the initial futures price on day 0 is $100, the initial margin requirement is 5%, the maintenance margin requirement is 3%, the settlement price on day 1 is $99.2, the settlement price on day 2 is $96, and the settlement price on day 3 is $101?

   *A. $40 = $50 + $8 + $32 - $50; where 50 is the initial deposit, $8 is the gain on day 1, $32 is the gain on day 2, and $50 is the loss on day 3; the ending balances days 0 through 3 are $50, $58, $90, and $40
   B. $90
   C. $100

94. An investor goes long one futures contract at $50 with 2 days to expiration. The settlement price 1 day before expiration is $52 and the mark to market profit is $2. The settlement price at expiration is $53. How is the futures contract terminated by closeout?

   A. Receive $53 - $52 = $1
   B. Pay $52, receive asset worth $53
   *C. Sell contract at $53 for a mark to market profit of $53 - $52 = $1

Afternoon Exam

95. What has a specified rate for the exercise rate and a variable rate for the underlying rate?

   A. Put option
   B. Call option
   *C. Interest rate option

96. An asset manager enters into a $100 million equity swap and agrees to pay a dealer the return on a stock index and the dealer agrees to pay a fixed rate of 4%. Payments are made semi-annually based on 180 days out of a 365-day year. The value of the stock index starts at 280. In six months, the stock index is at 250. Which party pays what amount after the payments are netted?

   *A. The dealer pays the asset manager about $13 million = $100,000,000(4%)(180/365) - $100,000,000(250/280 - 1)
   B. The dealer pays the asset manager about $9 million
   C. The asset manager pays the dealer about $9 million

97. What does an indenture set forth?

   A. The rights of the issuer and the bondholders
   B. The rights of the issuer and the promises of the bondholders
   *C. The promises of the issuer and the rights of the bondholders

98. Which imbedded option is least likely to be considered an advantage to the issuer?

   A. Call provision
   B. Cap on a floater
   *C. Conversion privilege

99. Which bond most likely has the least interest rate risk?

   *A. Floating rate bond
   B. Zero-coupon bond
   C. 2% fixed coupon bond

100. Which is closest to the duration of a bond if the current price is 90, the price if yields decline by 25 basis points is 92.7, and the price if yields rise by 25 basis points is 88?

   A. 5.20
   B. 10.40
   *C. 10.44 = (92.7 - 88.0) / [2 (90)(.0025)]

Afternoon Exam

101. Which is least likely to be considered credit risk?

    A. Default risk
    *B. Inflation risk
    C. Downgrade risk

102. What are created by stripping the coupons and principal payments from Treasury securities?

    A. TIPS
    B. Notes
    *C. Zero-coupon Treasury instruments

103. What are bonds escrowed or collateralized by Treasury securities?

    A. Insured bonds
    B. Revenue bonds
    *C. Prefunded bonds

104. Which tools of the Federal Reserve are used most often?

    *A. Engaging in open market operations and changing the discount rate
    B. Engaging in open market operations and changing the bank reserve requirements
    C. Changing the bank reserve requirements and verbal persuasion to influence how bankers supply credit

105. If the ratio of the yield between two bonds is 1.1 and the yield on the higher quality bond is 5%, which is closest to the yield on the lower quality bond?

    A. 4.5%
    *B. 5.5% = 5% (1.1)
    C. 6.5%

106. Which is closest to the value of a 5-year 7% coupon bond with a maturity value of $100 discounted for a 5% annual discount rate on a semiannual basis?

    *A. $108.75; where n = 10, i = 2.5, PMT = 3.5, FV = 100, resulting in PV = -108.75;
    B. $112.10
    C. $115.44

Afternoon Exam

107. If the spot rates on an annual basis are 3.0% for 6 months, 3.3% for 1 year, and 3.5% for 1.5 years, which is closest to the price of a $100 par, 3.5% coupon 1.5-year Treasury security?

   A. $98
   B. $99
   *C. $100 = 1.75 / 1.015 + 1.75 / 1.0165^2 + 101.75 / 1.0175^3

108. For an 8% option-free bond, the price changes by 3% if the rates rise 50 basis points. What is the change if rates fall by 50 basis points?

   A. Less than 3%
   B. Exactly 3%
   *C. More than 3%

109. How good is an estimated new price using duration likely to be for a 10 basis point increase in yield?

   *A. Estimated price close to new price
   B. Overestimates new price by over 10%
   C. Underestimates new price by over 10%

110. Which is closest to percentage price change for a bond with modified duration of 6.5 and convexity of -42.4 if yields increase by 200 basis points?

   *A. -14.70% = -6.5 (.02) - 42.4 (.02)^2
   B. -13.42%
   C. -6.92%

111. Which is least likely to be considered a disadvantage of exchange-traded funds (ETFs)?

   A. Transparency
   B. Cost-effectiveness
   *C. Narrow bid-ask spreads

112. Which is least accurate regarding real estate investments?

   A. Illiquid
   *B. Low transaction costs and high market efficiencies
   C. Not directly comparable to other properties, only approximately comparable

Afternoon Exam

113. Which is most accurate regarding real estate appraisals?

    A. Real estate appraisals show frequent changes
    *B. An appraisal-based index understates volatility
    C. A spuriously low volatility decreases the attractiveness of real estate

114. Which characteristic is least accurate in describing distressed-securities investing?

    A. The possibility of alpha from mispricing
    *B. Liquid with short-term commitment period
    C. Requires intense investor participation and consulting

115. Which investment strategy is most appropriate for building retirement or college education funds?

    A. Current income
    B. Capital preservation
    *C. Capital appreciation

116. Which countries had the highest equity allocations in pension fund portfolios in 1998?

    A. Japan and Germany
    B. Ireland and the United States
    *C. Hong Kong and the United Kingdom

117. What is the correlation coefficient if the covariance is 0.06%, and the standard deviations of the two individual return indexes are 2% and 3%?

    A. -1
    B. 0
    *C. 1 = 0.06% / [(2%)(3%)]

118. Which is closest to the standard deviation of a portfolio with a 60% weight in a security with an expected return of 10% and a standard deviation of 3%, and a 40% weight in a security with an expected return of 15% and a standard deviation of 5%, if the correlation coefficient is 1.00?

    A. 3.0%
    B. 3.6%
    *C. 3.8% = [(60%^2)(3%^2) + (40%^2)(5%^2) + 2(60%)(40%)(1.00)(3%)(5%)]^.5

Afternoon Exam

119. Which statement about portfolio risk and diversification is least accurate?

    A. Systematic risk cannot be eliminated through diversification
    B. Unsystematic risk can be significantly reduced through diversification
    *C. Diversification results from combining securities with perfect correlations

120. If the risk free rate is 5%, the return on the market portfolio is 9%, beta is -0.30, the current stock price is $50, and the expected price in one year is $53, the stock is

    A. Overvalued
    *B. Undervalued; 5% + (-0.30)(9% - 5%) = 3.80% < ($53 / $50) - 1 = 6.00%
    C. Properly valued

1. A. B. C.	41. A. B. C.	81. A. B. C.
2. A. B. C.	42. A. B. C.	82. A. B. C.
3. A. B. C.	43. A. B. C.	83. A. B. C.
4. A. B. C.	44. A. B. C.	84. A. B. C.
5. A. B. C.	45. A. B. C.	85. A. B. C.
6. A. B. C.	46. A. B. C.	86. A. B. C.
7. A. B. C.	47. A. B. C.	87. A. B. C.
8. A. B. C.	48. A. B. C.	88. A. B. C.
9. A. B. C.	49. A. B. C.	89. A. B. C.
10. A. B. C.	50. A. B. C.	90. A. B. C.
11. A. B. C.	51. A. B. C.	91. A. B. C.
12. A. B. C.	52. A. B. C.	92. A. B. C.
13. A. B. C.	53. A. B. C.	93. A. B. C.
14. A. B. C.	54. A. B. C.	94. A. B. C.
15. A. B. C.	55. A. B. C.	95. A. B. C.
16. A. B. C.	56. A. B. C.	96. A. B. C.
17. A. B. C.	57. A. B. C.	97. A. B. C.
18. A. B. C.	58. A. B. C.	98. A. B. C.
19. A. B. C.	59. A. B. C.	99. A. B. C.
20. A. B. C.	60. A. B. C.	100. A. B. C.
21. A. B. C.	61. A. B. C.	101. A. B. C.
22. A. B. C.	62. A. B. C.	102. A. B. C.
23. A. B. C.	63. A. B. C.	103. A. B. C.
24. A. B. C.	64. A. B. C.	104. A. B. C.
25. A. B. C.	65. A. B. C.	105. A. B. C.
26. A. B. C.	66. A. B. C.	106. A. B. C.
27. A. B. C.	67. A. B. C.	107. A. B. C.
28. A. B. C.	68. A. B. C.	108. A. B. C.
29. A. B. C.	69. A. B. C.	109. A. B. C.
30. A. B. C.	70. A. B. C.	110. A. B. C.
31. A. B. C.	71. A. B. C.	111. A. B. C.
32. A. B. C.	72. A. B. C.	112. A. B. C.
33. A. B. C.	73. A. B. C.	113. A. B. C.
34. A. B. C.	74. A. B. C.	114. A. B. C.
35. A. B. C.	75. A. B. C.	115. A. B. C.
36. A. B. C.	76. A. B. C.	116. A. B. C.
37. A. B. C.	77. A. B. C.	117. A. B. C.
38. A. B. C.	78. A. B. C.	118. A. B. C.
39. A. B. C.	79. A. B. C.	119. A. B. C.
40. A. B. C.	80. A. B. C.	120. A. B. C.

1. A. B. C.	41. A. B. C.	81. A. B. C.
2. A. B. C.	42. A. B. C.	82. A. B. C.
3. A. B. C.	43. A. B. C.	83. A. B. C.
4. A. B. C.	44. A. B. C.	84. A. B. C.
5. A. B. C.	45. A. B. C.	85. A. B. C.
6. A. B. C.	46. A. B. C.	86. A. B. C.
7. A. B. C.	47. A. B. C.	87. A. B. C.
8. A. B. C.	48. A. B. C.	88. A. B. C.
9. A. B. C.	49. A. B. C.	89. A. B. C.
10. A. B. C.	50. A. B. C.	90. A. B. C.
11. A. B. C.	51. A. B. C.	91. A. B. C.
12. A. B. C.	52. A. B. C.	92. A. B. C.
13. A. B. C.	53. A. B. C.	93. A. B. C.
14. A. B. C.	54. A. B. C.	94. A. B. C.
15. A. B. C.	55. A. B. C.	95. A. B. C.
16. A. B. C.	56. A. B. C.	96. A. B. C.
17. A. B. C.	57. A. B. C.	97. A. B. C.
18. A. B. C.	58. A. B. C.	98. A. B. C.
19. A. B. C.	59. A. B. C.	99. A. B. C.
20. A. B. C.	60. A. B. C.	100. A. B. C.
21. A. B. C.	61. A. B. C.	101. A. B. C.
22. A. B. C.	62. A. B. C.	102. A. B. C.
23. A. B. C.	63. A. B. C.	103. A. B. C.
24. A. B. C.	64. A. B. C.	104. A. B. C.
25. A. B. C.	65. A. B. C.	105. A. B. C.
26. A. B. C.	66. A. B. C.	106. A. B. C.
27. A. B. C.	67. A. B. C.	107. A. B. C.
28. A. B. C.	68. A. B. C.	108. A. B. C.
29. A. B. C.	69. A. B. C.	109. A. B. C.
30. A. B. C.	70. A. B. C.	110. A. B. C.
31. A. B. C.	71. A. B. C.	111. A. B. C.
32. A. B. C.	72. A. B. C.	112. A. B. C.
33. A. B. C.	73. A. B. C.	113. A. B. C.
34. A. B. C.	74. A. B. C.	114. A. B. C.
35. A. B. C.	75. A. B. C.	115. A. B. C.
36. A. B. C.	76. A. B. C.	116. A. B. C.
37. A. B. C.	77. A. B. C.	117. A. B. C.
38. A. B. C.	78. A. B. C.	118. A. B. C.
39. A. B. C.	79. A. B. C.	119. A. B. C.
40. A. B. C.	80. A. B. C.	120. A. B. C.